Studies in development and planning

This series consists of studies written by staff members of the Centre for Development Planning of the Erasmus University Rotterdam and by others specialized in the field of development and planning. This field includes, in broad terms, methods and techniques of development planning, analysis of and policies for development, economic policies towards developing countries, as well as the economics of centrally planned systems.

Most of the studies employ a quantitative approach. The common objective of all studies in this series is to contribute, directly or indirectly, to the formulation of policies that aim at furthering the fundamental goals of socioeconomic development, at regional, national, multinational, and global level. The editors express the hope that this broad objective may be reflected in the diversity of contributions to this series.

STUDIES IN DEVELOPMENT AND PLANNING

11

ALLOCATION
OF INDUSTRY
IN THE ANDEAN
COMMON MARKET

Jan ter Wengel

Professor of Economics
Javeriana University
Bogotá, Colombia
South America

Martinus Nijhoff Publishing
Boston / The Hague / London

Distributors for North America:
Martinus Nijhoff Publishing
Kluwer Boston, Inc.
160 Old Derby Street
Hingham, Massachusetts 02043

Distributors outside North America:
Kluwer Academic Publishers Group
Distribution Centre
P.O. Box 322
3300 AH Dordrecht, The Netherlands

Library of Congress Cataloging in Publication Data

Wengel, Jan ter.
  Allocation of industry in the Andean Common
Market.

  (Studies in development and planning; v. 11)
  Bibliography: p.
  1. Andes region – Industries. 2. Import
substitution – Andes region. 3. Acuerdo de
Cartagena. I. Title. II. Series: Studies
in development and planning (Rotterdam); v. 11.
HC167.A5W45   338'.098   79-18656
ISBN 0-89838-020-0

Printed in the United States of America.

CONTENTS

LIST OF TABLES

ACKNOWLEDGMENTS

There are several people I especially want to thank because of their direct contributions to this work and/or their indirect contribution by way of their support and encouragement during the time I wrote this study. Foremost among them are professors Alfred J. Field, Dennis R. Appleyard, and James L. Murphy, of the University of North Carolina at Chapel Hill, who read the various versions of this work and helped me identify the problems to be resolved as I progressed through the various versions. Further, I wish to thank Professors Ann D. Witte and Steven S. Rosefielde of the above mentioned university. I also wish to thank professor L.B.M. Mennes of the Centre for Development Planning, Erasmus University Rotterdam, for additional comments on this study. Finally I want to thank my parents whose contribution is too great to describe.

ALLOCATION
OF INDUSTRY
IN THE ANDEAN
COMMON MARKET

1 INTRODUCTION

The objective of this text is to develop and implement a model for allocating the industries of the Sectorial Programs of Industrial Development of the Andean Common Market. In the Andean Common Market, as in most other integration schemes among less developed countries, the main expectations regarding the promotion of economic growth are based on the expectation of increased opportunities for import substituting industrialization. The concern here is with the Andean Common Market in particular because it has been the economic integration scheme that has most explicitly recognized the objective of the less developed countries of taking advantage of the new opportunities for industrialization created by the combination of the individual markets. In the Andean Common Market the importance attached to the expectation of the gains from industrialization was expressed in the formulation of Sectorial Programs of Industrial Development. Other integration schemes among less developed countries have not addressed the issue of import substituting industrialization in such detailed manner.

In the first section of this chapter the importance of the topic of allocating industries in integration schemes among less developed countries is discussed. It is argued that the benefits to be derived from increased trade in the traditional products of the member countries are minimal. Instead, the member countries

1

expect the benefits from economic integration schemes to be derived from the utilization of the opportunities for industrialization created by such schemes.

The second section of this chapter is devoted to a description of the objectives and tools of the Cartagena Agreement, the treaty establishing the Andean Common Market. In the description of the Andean Common Market the importance of the Sectorial Programs of Industrial Development will be emphasized. The discussion will run parallel to that of Section I in demonstrating the relative unimportance of the trade liberalization measures with respect to that of the industrial allocation schemes.

In the last section of this chapter the organization of this study is presented. The elements of the model designed to allocate the industries of the Sectorial Programs of Industrial Development are described. Also the steps necessary for the implementation of the model in terms of data requirements and computational procedures are delineated.

Many less developed countries are interested in economic integration primarily as a means of fostering economic growth. Although the concern of the countries with economic integration is not always limited solely to the economic benefits of such schemes, the possible political and social objectives are not considered here. The participation in economic integration schemes is anticipated to foster economic growth through the creation of opportunities for more trade among the member countries in the products traditionally traded and through the creation of new opportunities for import substituting industrialization.

The possibilities of greater trade in traditional products among the member countries do not, however, promise to be as rewarding as the new opportunities for industrialization. In fact the economic benefits to be derived from the possibilities of greater trade are expected to be small. This result can be predicted with the traditional customs union theory developed by Viner[1] and others. This theory, which is otherwise of very limited use in the analysis of the economic integration schemes among less developed countries,[2] affirms that the gains from integration are equal to the difference between the trade creation and trade diversion effects resulting from the creation of a customs union. Countries stand to gain the most from economic integration schemes when their trade with third countries is limited while the trade among themselves is important. In such cases the reduction of tariffs among the member countries will lead to trade creation without propitiating losses through trade diversion. The theory developed by Viner and his successors also demonstrates that the extent of the benefits derivable from integration are proportional to the extent of the reduction in the prices resulting from the elimination of tariffs: the higher the pre-integration tariffs, the greater the benefits. In less developed countries the benefits to be derived from increased intra-area trade are expected to be small because the trade conditions among the LDCs entering into integration agreements are often exactly the opposite of the conditions postulated in customs union theory for maximum benefits. Often the bulk of the trade of the countries entering such integration agreements is with the rest of the world and only a small fraction of the external trade of these countries is with the prospective economic union members. The less developed countries usually trade with third countries rather than with each other because LDCs are generally exporters of primary products. In addition to the fact that they export primary products, the gains from the trade liberalization for these products are small because these products are traditionally not taxed heavily in international trade. In turn the less developed countries are primarily interested in importing capital and intermediate goods that are usually not produced in the other less developed countries either. Thus, in general, the less developed countries trade very little with each other and therefore, as indicated by traditional customs union theory, the LDCs stand to gain very little from the trade creation effect resulting from the formation of customs unions.

In contrast to the negligible gains to be derived from the expansion of trade by the reduction of intra-area tariffs, the promotion of import substituting industrialization is anticipated to be an influential element in promoting the growth of the member countries. Although in essence the production in the area of erstwhile imported products is trade diverting, the participating countries expect the benefits of domestic production to outweigh the losses due to trade diversion. The gains in income expected are anticipated to result from greater investment, better utilization of productive factors, external economies of production, and the relaxation of balance of payments problems. The participating countries expect these gains to outweigh the losses due to trade diversion as predicted by customs union theory within a static framework. Traditional customs union theory does not consider the case of the dynamic benefits to be derived from industrialization.

Traditional customs union theory also has very little to say about the distribution of the gains from economic integration schemes. Although the issue of the distribution of the static benefits may not be significant because of the un-importance of these benefits in integration schemes among less developed countries, the issue of the distribution of the gains from industrialization cannot be overlooked. The less developed countries entering into customs union arrangements expect the benefits from such unions to be in the form of industries locating within their borders.

The sanguine expectations for import substituting industrialization do not ensure that all member countries will participate in the new industries. Without adequate means for redistributing the gains from import substituting industrialization such as lump sum transfers, the main distributive issue concerns the location of industries: countries expect to gain from industries locating within their borders. Thus the distributional issue to be resolved is that of the determination of the locations of the new industries.

The determination of the location of industries is not left to the market because the relatively less developed of the members entering into economic integration arrangements fear that the new industries will tend to concentrate in the relatively more advanced countries. Their fears are based on the theories of development poles that propose that industries will tend to locate in places that offer adequate infrastructures. The relatively less developed countries fear that the regional disparities will be enhanced rather than dissipated.[3]

In order to ensure that all the members of economic integration arrangements participate in the new industries, provisions regarding the locations of industries may be made in integration agreements. These provisions, sometimes denominated complementation agreements, are designed to determine the locations of new industries.

In the Andean Common Market the industrial location provisions were not limited in scope. Rather, the recognition of the importance of the benefits to be derived from industrialization prompted the formulation of extensive and detailed Sectorial Programs of Industrial Development. These programs, designed for selected sectors and selected industries within the chosen sectors, aim to assign industries equitably to all member countries.

In the Andean Common Market, although there are few problems in the selection of the sectors to be considered for such programs and of the industries to be included in such programs, the problem of the allocation of the industries of the programs has proved a major stumbling block to the implementation of the Sectorial Programs of Industrial Development. The selection of sectors for programs of industrial development and the selection of the industries to be included do not directly affect any of the members and therefore these two steps in the formulation of the Sectorial Programs of Industrial Development are fairly easy. The allocation of industries within these programs determines the benefits to be derived by the member countries and proves much more difficult.

Therefore one of the main problems to be resolved in integration schemes among developing countries is that of the allocation of the new industries that are made possible by the enlarged market. In the complementation agreements of some economic integration schemes and in the Sectorial Programs of Industrial Development of the Andean Common Market the industries to be allocated were assigned to the countries on the basis of negotiations. Thus, the countries negotiated specific allocation schemes. The problem is that there is no assurance that such negotiated solutions are optimal and that they allocate the industries in such a manner as to minimize the costs of the goods to be produced. Furthermore the solutions are hard to achieve because the negotiations are difficult due to a lack of consensus regarding the exact benefits provided by different industries.

Nevertheless, in practice the negotiated solutions might still be preferable to those theoretically possible with the usual optimizing methods. The determination of the optimal locations of industries usually requires the minimization of the costs of allocating different industries to different countries. The design of such an allocation is impossible in practice, however, because of the lack of complete data on the costs of all goods and factors in all countries.

The objective of this text is to develop a model that will allocate the industries of the Sectorial Programs of Industrial Development on the basis of costs, but that will not be subject to the shortcomings of the other approaches, since the determination of those costs will be circumvented. Thus, a method will be designed that will not suffer from the data constraints imposed by the usual optimizing models and that at the same time will presumably be superior to the negotiated solution in producing an approximately optimal solution.

II

During the 1960s the United Nations' Economic Commission for Latin America favored Latin American integration because it claimed that import substitution on a national level had run its course by the mid-1950s. This doctrine served as the rationale for Latin American economic integration and the ratification of the Montevideo Treaty that established the Latin American Free Trade Association (LAFTA) composed of Argentina, Brazil, Chile, Paraguay, Peru, Uruguay, and Mexico. The group was later joined by Bolivia, Colombia, Ecuador, and Venezuela.

The market functioned normally during the first few years after its inception and the only change was that the traditional bilateral arrangements were multilateralized in accordance with the most favored nation clause. However, it soon became evident that the middle income group countries, later labelled "insufficient market" countries—Colombia, Chile, Peru, Uruguay, and Venezuela—were not able to compete with the "industrial giants"—Argentina, Brazil, and Mexico. Further, even though granted special concessions, the poorer members of the group—Bolivia, Ecuador, and Paraguay—also felt that they were getting few if any benefits from the integration scheme and were in fact "running the risk of becoming markets for the industrial surplus of the 'big three'."[4] The differences between the three groups with respect to distributional issues were not resolved and the progress in the negotiation of trade liberalization agreements stagnated. The members publicly acknowledged their inability to proceed with the trade liberalization commitments of the Montevideo Treaty in their Caracas Protocol of December 1969.

Due to the dissatisfaction of the insufficient market countries with the benefits derived from LAFTA, these countries decided to form a subregional market within LAFTA that would improve their negotiating leverage. Thus, with the Declaration of Bogota of 1966 a committee was designed to formulate a project for a subregional market within LAFTA. The project was approved by Bolivia, Chile, Colombia, Ecuador, and Peru, and these countries subscribed to the Cartagena Agreement of 1969 that formally created the Andean Common Market. Venezuela which had cooperated in the preparation of the project for a subregional market did not join the Andean Common Market then but did so in 1973. Chile later seceded from the market in November 1976.

Although Chile seceded from the market in 1976 and rescinded from all obligations and benefits of the market, it was a participant in the Petrochemical Program of Industrial Development. In such capacity it cooperated in the design of the agreement and in the repartition of the industries of the program. Therefore Chile will be considered as a member in the analysis of the Petrochemical Program.

The Andean Common Market (ACM) was established as a group that would be more homogeneous than LAFTA and that would be large enough to be able to bargain effect: ly with the larger LAFTA members. The ACM covers 5,457,000 squa:e kilometers, which represents about a third of the total area of South America. Its population of 72.7 million is larger than that of Argentina (25.0 million) or Mexico (58.1 million) but smaller than that of Brazil (103.4 million) and represents about 25 percent of the population of Latin America. (These and subsequent figures are for 1974.) The gross national product of the group is 42 billion dollars, which is comparable to that of Brazil (54 billion) or Mexico (56 billion) and larger than that of Argentina (18 billion).[5]

In the Andean Common Market the country with the largest population is Colombia with 22.9 million. The country with the smallest population is Bolivia with 5.5 million. In between are Peru, Venezuela, Chile, and Ecuador with populations of 15.4, 11.6, 10.08, and 6.5 million respectively.[6]

Among the six countries Venezuela, with 13,519 million dollars per year, has the highest gross national product. It is followed by Colombia, Chile, and Peru with 8,750, 8,725, and 7,630 million dollars per year respectively. The relatively poorer countries, Ecuador and Bolivia, have gross national products of 2,086 and 1,265 million dollars per year respectively. In terms of per capita income Venezuela is again first with 1,165 dollars per capita per year. It is followed by Chile, Peru, and Colombia with 866, 495, and 382 dollars per capita per year respectively. Ecuador and Bolivia are again last with 321 and 230 dollars per capita per year.

The objectives for the formation of the Andean Common Market are stated in article 1 of the Cartagena Agreement as:

> The objectives of the present Agreement are to promote the balanced and harmonic development of the member countries, accelerate their growth by means of economic integration, facilitate their participation in the integration scheme established by the Treaty of Montevideo and establish favorable conditions for the conversion of LAFTA to a common market: all this with the purpose of procuring a lasting improvement in the level of living of the people of the subregion.[7]

From among the avowed goals of the Cartagena Agreement only the goal of the acceleration of economic growth can be regarded as practical. The goals of ameliorating the developmental differences between the member countries and of fostering the progress of LAFTA are not clearly specified and are therefore very difficult to implement.

The tools proposed in the Cartagena Agreement for the fulfillment of the objectives of the Andean Common Market are:

1. The harmonization of social and economic policies.
2. Joint industrial planning.
3. A program of trade liberalization.
4. The establishment of a minimum common external tariff to be subsequently replaced by a common external tariff.
5. Agricultural development programs.
6. The channeling of resources to provide for the necessary investments.
7. Physical integration.
8. Preferential treatment for Bolivia and Ecuador.

The most important of the tools described above are those relating to industrial planning, trade liberalization, the establishment of a common external tariff, and the formation of a corporation to channel investment resources. Industrial programming or planning is necessary for the promotion of import substituting industrialization and to ensure industrial complementation to avoid wasteful duplication. The industrial programs to be implemented were not spelled out in the original draft of the Cartagena Agreement but were to be developed later as Sectorial Programs of Industrial Development. The Trade Liberalization Program, spelled out in the original agreement, was designed to foster the reduction in the barriers to trade between the members. In order to eventually establish a Common External Tariff, the Cartagena Agreement proposed as an intermediate goal the establishment of a Minimum Common External Tariff. Neither the Minimum Common External Tariff or the Common External Tariff were spelled out in the original draft of the agreement and were left to posterior negotiation and implementation. The basis for the Andean Investment Corporation (corporacion Andina de Fomento) was established in the Agreement. The purpose of the Andean Investment Corporation is that of channeling resources for economic integration projects. The Andean Investment Corporation is also expected to study and identify new opportunities for such projects.

Although probably not as important as the four aforementioned tools of the Agreement for fostering the economic growth of the area, the prescription of a preferential treatment for Bolivia and Ecuador nevertheless merits attention. The prescription for a preferential treatment for Bolivia and Ecuador is relevant to the distributional aspects of the integration scheme.

The other tools for the promotion of the integration scheme proposed by the Agreement are judged by the author to be of limited importance. The objective of harmonizing social and economic policies has little practical relevance. Similarly, the goal of concerted agricultural programs is also judged to be unimportant in practice since the countries are expected to pursue independent agricultural policies and the participation of agricultural products in the trade among the member countries is minimal. Lastly, the objective of physical integration, if at all possible, could only be expected in the distant future.

In order to ensure the compliance with the norms of the Agreement and in order to promote the process of integration the Agreement has as principal institutions the Comite del Acuerdo de Cartagena and the Junta del Acuerdo de Cartagena. The Comite del Acuerdo de Cartagena is the governing body of the agreement and is responsible for the approval of all programs and policies to be implemented in the Andean Common Market. The Junta del Acuerdo de Cartagena (JUNAC) is the technical body of the agreement. It is responsible to the Comite, which determines the problems and programs to be studied.

The Cartagena Agreement paid special attention to distributional issues since one of the most important problems to be resolved in integration schemes among less developed countries is that of the distribution of benefits. The distributional problem arises from the fact that free trade and free markets have not always assured an acceptable distribution of the gains from such integration schemes: the relatively less developed members fear that the new industries will locate in the relatively more developed centers and thereby increase the disparity in development levels.[8] However, the Cartagena Agreement did not establish any desired distribution pattern with the consequence that the establishment of a Minimum Common External Tariff, the introduction of a Program of Trade Liberalization, the design of the form of the preferential treatment for Bolivia and Ecuador, and the allocation of industries within the Sectorial Programs of

Industrial Development — the measures that determine the distribution of benefits — were the result of intergovernmental bargaining rather than of economic analysis.[9] The actions of the Andean Investment Corporation are expected to conform to the distributive norms suggested by the implementation of the above stated programs.

The negotiation of the first three measures affecting the distribution of benefits presented relatively few problems. The achievement of an agreement on the Trade Liberalization Program designed to lower tariffs between the member countries offered no great difficulties because of the initial very limited trade between the countries and the generous lists of exceptions to the program allowed the member countries. The intraregional trade among the six countries amounted to only 3.5 percent of the total of the foreign trade of these countries in 1970.[10] Furthermore, the countries were allowed to exempt from the Trade Liberalization Program such products as they included in their exemption lists. In the exemption lists Chile, Colombia, and Venezuela could include 250 items; Peru was allowed to include 350; and Bolivia and Ecuador were permitted exemption lists including 650 products each. Given a very limited amount of trade and the possibility of restricting the trade of many products, it was anticipated that the benefits from trade liberalization would be very limited. Because of the relative unimportance of the benefits to be derived from the Trade Liberalization Program, agreement on the program was not difficult to achieve, the program was included in the Cartagena Agreement, and controversy with respect to the program was limited.

The initial integrationist spirit and the relative unimportance of the decisions also facilitated the adoption of a Minimum Common External Tariff. The tariffs of the member countries were generally higher than the agreed upon minimum and thus the negotiation of the Minimum Common External Tariff amounted to little more than an exercise in rational tariff setting in preparation for the Common External Tariff negotiations. The member countries have not been able to agree on a Common External Tariff and negotiations have stalled. The 100th Decision of the Comite del Acuerdo de Cartagena formally acknowledged the inability of the countries to reach an agreement on a Common External Tariff in the period designated in the Cartagena Agreement, and the objective of the establishment of the Common External Tariff was postponed.

The initial commitment to economic integration provided for the assignment to Bolivia and Ecuador of a set of industries not yet existent in the area. The assignment of these industries represents a one time concession granted to Bolivia and Ecuador in fulfillment of the commitment of a prescription for a preferential treatment for the relatively less developed countries.

The task of allocating the industries of the Sectorial Programs of Industrial Development proved more difficult. Although the countries readily agreed on the sectors to be selected for Sectorial Programs and on the industries to be included in these programs, they found it almost impossible to agree on the allocation of industries within the programs. The negotiations for the allocation of industries within these programs proved long and complicated and only two programs, those of the metal working and petrochemical industries have been ratified.[11] The negotiations for the allocations of the industries of the other Sectorial Programs of Industrial Development have stagnated. Other programs have not been approved because of the anticipated importance of the Sectorial Programs of Industrial Development in determining the development of the participating countries and the directions of trade among them. The industries included in these programs are those producing capital and intermediate goods and, therefore, they are expected to influence the development of the region. It is also expected that the future trade among the member countries will be concentrated in the products of these industries. Thus, it is anticipated that to a large extent the distribution of benefits will hinge on the particular allocation of industries within these programs.

The purpose of this study is to formulate a method for allocating the industries of the Sectorial Programs of Industrial Development. This method will be formulated because of the importance of the Sectorial Programs of Industrial Development in the determination of the progress of the integration scheme. Further, the development of such a method makes possible a more rational allocation of industries since the design of these allocations will no longer be based on negotiations but rather on economic principles.

III

The first two sections of this chapter demonstrated the need for the development of a practicable method for allocating the industries of the complementation agreements of integration schemes among less developed countries. In the next chapter it will be pointed out that such a method has not been developed. It will be pointed out that with respect to integration schemes among less developed countries very little attention has been paid to the subjects of the distribution of benefits in general and the allocation of industries in particular.

In Chapter III a practicable model is developed for the allocation of the industries of the Sectorial Programs of Industrial Development. In that chapter, some generally accepted investment criteria are discussed and a criterion, the domestic resource cost of foreign exchange, is selected as the appropriate criterion for allocation in a multi-country situation. Next, it is indicated that the domestic resource cost can be estimated from the effective rate of protection. The selected investment criterion is then employed to formulate the objective function of an integer programming model designed to allocate the industries of the Sectorial Programs of Industrial Development.

The model developed in Chapter III is implemented to determine the optimal allocation of industries of the petrochemical program of the Andean Common Market. In Chapter IV the petrochemical industry is described in order to provide a background for the analysis of the petrochemical program. Also the industrial allocation designed by the Junta del Acuerdo de Cartagena is delineated.

In Chapter V the domestic resource cost of foreign exchange for each of the industries in each of the countries is calculated. The calculation of the domestic resource costs requires a large amount of data. The nature, sources, and reliability of these data are discussed in Chapter V.

In Chapters VI and VII the model is implemented in order to devise optimal allocations of industries subject to a variety of distributional constraints. The model is implemented as a linear programming problem in Chapter VI and as an integer programming problem in Chapter VII. In these chapters the different industry allocations obtained by subjecting the model to different distributional constraints are compared. These industry allocations are also compared to the allocation of industries designed by the Junta del Acuerdo de Cartagena.

The main points of the study are summarized in Chapter VIII. The usefulness of the model for facilitating the formulation of Sectorial Programs of Industrial Development is discussed. Also the efficiency of the model in designing more economical allocations of industries is analyzed. Finally, some recommendations for further research are made.

2 PRINCIPAL CONTRIBUTIONS TO THE PROBLEMS OF DISTRIBUTION AND ALLOCATION

In the last chapter it was established that the purpose of this text is to design a method to allocate the industries of the Sectorial Programs of Industrial Development of the Andean Common Market among the member countries in a manner acceptable to all. The purpose of this chapter is to describe briefly the progress that has been made toward the solution of the problem of the assignment of industries in integration schemes among less developed countries. The review of the literature marking this progress will be limited to the following:

1. The description of the main approaches suggested for distributing the benefits of integration arrangements among less developed countries.
2. The delineation of the schemes proposed for the resolution of the industry allocation problem.

The literature reviewed here is limited specifically to the topics outlined above because of the broadness of the areas touched upon in the analysis of the equitable allocation problem. The contributions in the areas of the theory of customs unions, location theory, and investment planning not directly related to the problem at hand will not be discussed.

The theory of customs unions is not examined here because of its limited relevance to the objectives of the less developed countries. As pointed out by Cooper and Massell, for customs union theory to be applicable to LDCs it should "focus on economies of scale, changes in the terms of trade, balance of payments problems, externalities, capital imports, and underemployment."[1] Indeed, they went further to state that "a principal objective of economic integration among less developed countries is to foster industrial development and to guide such development along more economic lines."[2] Thus, Cooper and Massell indicated that the rationale for economic integration among LDCs was based on dynamic rather than static factors and that therefore customs union theory was of limited relevance.[3]

As pointed out by Robson, "The theory was evolved with the cases of Benelux, European integration, and thus, the more developed countries in mind,"[4] and is concerned mainly with the static gains to be achieved through the reallocation of the existing resources. Thus, the theory has limited relevance to less developed countries since "their arguments for integration are basically concerned with its contribution to economic growth and the structural transformation of less developed countries,"[5] and the "actual trade flows and the actual degree of competitiveness or complementarity are regarded as largely irrelevant."[6] The limited applicability of the theory of customs unions to integration schemes among less developed countries is further indicated in Jaber's review article titled "The Relevance of Traditional Integration Theory to Less Developed Countries."[7] In it Jaber states that "the main concern of the traditional theory of economic integration is to evaluate the desirability of a customs union from the world's welfare viewpoint using static effects as criteria."[8] He further points out that "most writers feel that the traditional theory of economic integration has limited relevance, if any, to LDCs,"[9] and that:

1. "Economic integration in case of the LDCs should be treated as an approach to economic development rather than as a tariff issue."[10]
2. "The emphasis should be put on dynamic rather than static effects in evaluating the desirability of economic integration among LDCs."[11]

Industrial location theory is not reviewed here because it "is abstract and for the most part does not bear directly on the problems with which regional analysts and planners are concerned."[12] A review of this literature is presented by Nixson in his book titled *Economic Integration and Industrial Location: An East African Case Study.*[13] Nixson's book presents "an attempt to comprehend in its totality the dynamic interaction between industrial location and economic integration in East Africa. . . . Inevitably, this involves a consideration of economic, political and historical forces."[14] However, the "study is neither an assessment of costs and benefits, nor an analysis and description of industrial location per se"[15] and therefore does not provide any indication as to how to allocate industries in integration schemes among less developed countries.

It must be noted however that the model developed in the next chapter for the allocation of industries in the Andean Common Market is based on a procedure basic to location theory, the comparative cost technique. Isard describes the objectives and basis for a study utilizing this technique as follows:

> A comparative cost study typically proceeds for any given industry on the basis of an established or anticipated pattern of markets and a given geographic distribution of raw materials and other productive factors used in the industry. The objective of the study is to determine in what region or regions the industry could achieve the lowest total cost of producing and delivering its product to the market.[16]

This technique, which serves as a basis for several of the industry assignment studies reviewed in Section II, is extended in Chapter III to cover many industries in several countries.

A review of the planning literature is not attempted here for two reasons. First, the literature in this field is too extensive and the reader might best be referred to a discussion of planning theory such as that presented by Heal in *The Theory of Economic Planning*[17] and to a discussion of planning models such as that presented by Taylor in Blitzer, Clark, and Taylor's *Economy-Wide Models and Development Planning*.[18] Second, the goals of planning are usually macroeconomic in character and the planning models are too aggregative in nature to provide any indication as to how to allocate particular industries in particular countries.

Although too aggregative to provide guidelines for the allocation of industries in the Andean Common Market, the study by Mennes, *Planning Economic Integration Among Developing Countries*,[19] nevertheless merits attention because of its close relationship to the topic at hand. The purpose of Mennes' book is to present a planning formulation that minimizes investment costs given target income increases for each of two countries taken separately and for the two countries taken together in an economic integration framework. The target income increases lead to increases in the demands for the products of the various sectors of the two economies and the objective of the model is to minimize the investment outlays for the required corresponding capacity increases. As indicated by Mennes, this model could also be formulated to maximize income subject to savings constraints. Although Mennes extends his analysis to cover "large projects," his approach "only makes sense if there is a reasonable expectation that the projects' effects on total economic activity will be considerable. If not, sectoral or even cost-benefit analysis is appropriate."[20] A number of industry allocation schemes designed on the basis of cost-benefit analysis are presented in Section II of this chapter and additional comments on cost-benefit analysis are made in Chapter III, since the model proposed for allocating industries is also based on this type of analysis.

Although the problem of the allocation of industries in integration schemes among less developed countries bears on several different areas, it does not fit very well into any of these areas and therefore no extensive review of the literature of any of these areas is presented. The literature reviewed in the next two sections is that specifically concerned with the issues of the distribution of benefits and of the allocation of industries in such integration schemes. In the first section the distributional provisions of several economic integration arrangements are presented. The practicality of these distributional provisions is discussed in view of the historical experience of the integration arrangements in question and the comments on the subject presented in the literature. In the second section of this chapter various models proposed for allocating industries are discussed and their limitations in practice are described.

I

The purpose of this section is to review the most relevant instruments that can be utilized to distribute the gains of integration schemes among less developed countries. To achieve this goal the distributional tools utilized in the Central American Common Market (CACM), the Latin American Free Trade Association (LAFTA), the Central African Customs and Economic Union (UDEAC), and the East African Common Market (EACM) will be discussed.[21] Next, some general considerations with respect to the distribution of benefits presented in the literature will be described.

The theory of customs unions has very limited relevance for integration schemes among less developed countries. "A further reason for qualifying the traditional theory is that it takes no account of the way in which the potential benefits from integration may be distributed among the member countries."[22] The lack of attention paid to the issue of distribution is probably the result of the fact that the theory of customs unions was developed with the case of the economic integration of Europe in mind.

The objectives of the Rome and Paris Treaties establishing the European Common Market[23] were to remove the barriers to trade, to increase competition, and to give a freer reign to market forces. Thus McLachlan and Swann state that "one of the most obvious aims of both treaties is the removal of trade barriers such as customs, duties, quotas, and so on, between member states so as to establish free trade."[24] With the removal of these barriers to trade "the general level of productive efficiency would rise"[25] because "the inefficient (producers) would be faced with competition from more efficient outsiders."[26] Therefore, "both treaties seek to bring about a competitive order because it is held that competition will guarantee something approaching the optimum allocation of resources."[27] Nevertheless it must be noted that there are slight differences between the treaties in that "the authors of the Rome Treaty provided no other form of guidance and control,"[28] while the Paris Treaty enables "the High Authority to apply price floors and ceilings, production quotas, and consumption priorities."[29] However, in spite of the greater powers conferred the High Authority by the Paris Treaty, the use of these powers has generally been limited to the checking of such forces as would limit competition.

Corresponding to the commitment to the market the Rome and Paris Treaties did not consider the issue of the distribution of the benefits from integration among the member countries. Indeed, although it may be argued that the regulation of some industries has distributive implications, the objectives of these regulations are not distributive in nature. The regulated industries in question are the transport, agricultural, and coal industries. The basic reasons for the regulation of the transport industry were to create an efficient transportation system and to eliminate the market distortions that existed in the various countries because of the legacy of the governments' interventions in transportation problems.[30] The objectives for intervention in agriculture were to unify the market conditions in the area, to promote structural reform, and to mitigate the discrepancy between industrial and agricultural incomes.[31] The purpose for the regulation of the coal industry was to assure coal supplies indiscriminately to all members and to mitigate the long-term dependence on foreign energy sources.[32]

The regulation of two of the above mentioned industries, agriculture and the coal industry, however, had strong distributional implications. Thus, agriculture was regulated because "states such as France and the Netherlands felt that a community based purely on free trade in industrial goods would be one-sided."[33] The European Common Market in part chose to promote the coal industry by means of subsidies rather than by taxing alternate forms of energy in order to favor Italian industry.

The loans of the European Investment Bank also have an impact on the distribution of benefits in the area. Although the Bank was designed to help ameliorate the income discrepancies among regions that were not defined to coincide with general boundaries, the bulk of the loans have been made to Italy.[34]

It can be concluded that the European Common Market does not provide any clear guidelines regarding the distribution of benefits. Indeed, although mainly left to the market, the distribution of these benefits appears to have been altered haphazardly through the regulation of the agricultural and coal industries. Nevertheless, an institution such as the European Investment Bank could serve as an efficient means for improving the distribution of the benefits of integration schemes.

Among the integration arrangements among less developed countries the Central American Common Market (CACM) is presented first because it represents the one with the least distributive provisions. The Central American Common Market was formed in 1958 by Costa Rica, El Salvador, Guatemala, Honduras, and Nicaragua.

> The major objectives (of CACM) were five in number: (1) intraregional freedom of trade; (2) equalization of external tariffs; (3) harmonization of policies to promote industrialization; (4) encouragement of local industries to supply the regional market; and (5) freedom of movement for factors of production within the region.[35]

The Central American Common Market foundered on the issue of the distribution of benefits from integration. Thus the third and fourth objectives of the market, presented in the last paragraph, were designed to eliminate production and export subsidies, dumping and national preferences for public purchases and not to dictate industrial location or the distribution of benefits. Indeed the original treaty did not even consider the issues of the equalization of fiscal incentives and permitted an "initial free-for-all to attract foreign industrial investment."[36] An agreement on integration industries in which countries would be assigned particular industries was introduced later but "problems in negotiating agreements (respecting the assignments of industries to countries) have held up the complicated scheme."[37] Finally, although the CACM had a Bank for Economic Integration, it was not used to pursue distributive goals and its loans were granted about equally to all members.[38]

The second integration scheme presented here is the Latin American Free Trade Association (LAFTA). This association was established by the Montevideo Treaty of 1960 signed by Argentina, Brazil, Chile, Mexico, Paraguay, Peru, and Uruguay. It was later joined by Colombia, Ecuador, Venezuela, and Bolivia and was designed with the following objectives:

1. A program of trade liberalization spanning 12 years, intended to free items of intrazonal trade of all restriction by member countries. Such trade items were classed in two categories for purposes of liberalization procedure: (a) a "National List" of items toward which members agreed on annual reductions of duty and/or other restriction, and (b) a "Common List" of items of current trade to be fully freed of restriction, in any event, by no later than 1973.

2. The goal of expanded intrazonal trade and of greater economic complementarity within the region.
3. Retention of a most-favored-nation clause, assuring the extension of liberalization benefits to all member countries.
4. Provision for internal taxation on imports no less favorable than that accorded similar national products.
5. Retention of "escape clauses," enabling a country to restrict importation whenever a given product "threatens" the national economy.
6. Special provisions on behalf of agriculture.
7. Special provisions aimed at allaying fears of "lesser developed" member countries of economic inundation within a regional context.
8. Institutions and administrative organs: a Conference of Contracting Parties and Executive Committee, an intrazonal payments system, and a Council of Ministers to head LAFTA beginning in 1966.[39]

Although the arrangement initially led to an increase in trade, trade later declined.[40] Furthermore, the tariff concessions granted on the National Lists by the various countries became less numerous every year. The slowdown in the progress of LAFTA was accompanied by a growing dissatisfaction among the relatively less developed countries, which perceived that they were becoming markets for the industrial giants, Argentina, Brazil, and Mexico, while they themselves were gaining little from the arrangement. In time the trade liberalization negotiations stagnated and the members acknowledged their inability to proceed with the trade liberalization commitments of the Montevideo Treaty in their Caracas Protocol of 1969.

Although one of the provisions of LAFTA demonstrated the objective of giving preferential treatment to the lesser developed countries, the practical implementation of this provision did little to solve the problems of these countries. The fact that these countries were permitted to reduce tariffs at a slower rate than the relatively more developed countries provided no help: the industrial giants already produced the products that the lesser developed countries could produce, and the only benefit gained from a slower rate of tariff reductions was that the domestic markets remained protected for a longer period of time. The easiest way in which the relatively less developed countries could be favored within LAFTA would be through the implementation of complementation agreements. These agreements, however, proved very difficult to negotiate and only a few such agreements dealing with relatively unimportant industries have been signed.[41]

The policy tools suggested by the LAFTA agreement for improving the distribution of benefits are rate of tariff reduction concessions and complementation agreements. The effect of the first is very limited and the second, although more promising, is hampered by the difficulty of negotiating these agreements.

The third integration scheme among LDCs considered here is the Union Douaniere et Economique de l'Afrique Centrale (UDEAC) or Central African Economic and Customs Union.[42] This union is composed of Congo (Brazzaville), Gabon, the Central African Republic, Chad, and the Federal Republic of the Cameroon. A substantial measure of integration has existed between the first four since the establishment of the Federation of French Equatorial Africa. Although these countries sought independence separately they agreed to the formation of a customs union, Union Douaniere Equatoriale, in 1959. This group was joined in 1961 by the Federal Republic of Cameroon and finally UDEAC was formally established in 1964.

The principal method for affecting the distribution of the benefits from integration available to the UDEAC countries is that of the distribution of the revenues collected by the Solidarity Fund. The Solidarity Fund, in which all countries except Cameroon participate, collects 20 percent of all import duties regardless of the final destination of the goods; the other 80 percent of the duty is duly transferred to the country representing the final destination of the goods. The proceeds of the Solidarity Fund are distributed as follows: Chad 62 percent, Central African Republic 35 percent, and Congo 3 percent. Gabon's share is very small.[43] A second scheme proposed in UDEAC for influencing the distribution of benefits is that of industrial coordination. However, no specific framework was designed for this coordination because of a lack of agreement between the relatively more developed countries Cameroon, Gabon, and Congo and the relatively less developed Chad and Central African Republic. Thus,

> On the one hand, the view of Cameroon, Gabon, and to some extent, Congo was that there should be free competition for industrial development within an agreed framework of investment concessions. On the other hand, Chad and CAR (Central African Republic) insisted that since they would be unlikely to be able to attract industry in such a framework, account should be taken of their unfavorable position by the introduction of measures to influence the location of industry in the common market.[44]

The tools for improving the distribution of benefits within UDEAC are the distribution of the revenues of the Solidarity Fund and the proposed coordination of industrialization. The first of these policy tools appears not to provide sufficient compensation to Chad and the Central African Republic so that these countries propose the adoption of measures designed to influence the location of industry. However, although the member countries agreed to proposals calling for such measures no practical framework for allocating industries was developed and therefore the issue of industrial location has remained unsolved.

The last integration scheme among less developed countries considered here is the East African Common Market (EACM) composed of Kenya, Uganda, and Tanganyika, later Tanzania. EACM represents an economic integration scheme that dates back to 1917 when a customs union between Kenya and Uganda was established. Tanzania was brought into the union 10 years later.

In spite of its long standing "the distribution of benefits began to be a problem in the mid-to-late 1950s"[45] as Uganda and Tanzania feared that only Kenya was benefiting from the arrangement. In an attempt to improve the distribution of benefits a Distributable Pool was set up. The three countries would contribute to this pool 6 percent of their customs and excise collections and 40 percent of the yield of the income taxes charged to companies. The pool was to be distributed as follows: one half would go to the Common Services Organization (East African High Commission) and the other half would be distributed equally to the three countries.[46] The Distributable Pool scheme for fiscal redistribution did not solve the East Africa distributional problem as Kenya considered the income transfers to Uganda and Tanzania to be too large while the latter two considered the compensation paid by Kenya to be too small, and the Distributable Pool was subsequently dismantled.

The fiscal redistribution scheme of the East African Common Market failed partly because Uganda and Tanzania were not only interested in revenue but also wanted a larger share of the manufacturing activity in the area. In order to deal with this problem the Kampala-Mbale Agreements provided a set of measures designed to locate any expansion of existing industry in Uganda and Tanzania, and to locate new industries equitably among the members. The proposed measures for the determination of industrial location were never implemented since Kenya never ratified the Kampala-Mbale Agreements.

Given the failures of the fiscal redistribution and industry allocation schemes the East African Common Market faced possible dissolution. This was, however, stemmed by the Treaty for East African Cooperation of 1967. The distributive tools incorporated in this treaty are: (1) transfer taxes and (2) the East African Development Bank. Transfer taxes, a euphemism for tariffs, make it "possible for the industrially less developed countries to impose . . . tariffs on imports of manufacturers from the relatively more developed in order to protect their own manufacturing industries."[47] The East African Development Bank, established with an initial capital of £6 million subscribed to equally by the three countries, was designed to improve the distribution of benefits by lending 38.75 percent to Uganda and Tanzania respectively and only 22.50 percent to Kenya.

The tools employed for the distribution of benefits in the integration schemes among less developed countries described are the following:

1. Fiscal redistribution: UDEAC; EACM.

2. Development banks: CACM; EACM.
3. Retainment of tariff options: LAFTA; EACM.
4. Complementation agreements: CACM; LAFTA; UDEAC.
5. Allocation of industries: proposed for EACM.

The above mentioned tools will now be analyzed and the comments with respect to these tools presented in the literature will be noted.

In theory the benefits resulting from economic integration can best be distributed among the members through fiscal redistribution schemes. Thus, as pointed out by Morawetz:

> From a strictly theoretical viewpoint, and in a world of perfect information, no distortions, and no preference for industrial production, the optimal way of achieving benefit redistribution is through lump sum intergovernmental transfers.[48]

However, in the real world there is no perfect information, and in the less developed countries prices are very often distorted and there is generally a preference for industry. Therefore a fiscal redistribution plan is not practicable for two reasons. First, it is impossible to calculate the net benefits derived by the member countries from participation in the union. Second, given price distortions and a preference for industry, a fiscal redistribution "scheme is not necessarily the best (least-cost) way of achieving a given distribution of the benefits arising from union."[49]

In practice the main problem confronting fiscal redistribution schemes is that the participating countries may have different views on the appropriate prices to be applied in the calculation of the benefits. Hazelwood points out that because of the general preference for industry:

> It might be guessed that the transfers needed to make the loser think it was compensated would in most cases be larger than the aggregate gains from integration. At any rate, they would need to be larger than the payer would accept. No doubt there is an illogicality in these attitudes, but they nonetheless speak decisively against the adequacy of a system of fiscal transfers as a regulator of a common market.[50]

Mead also addressed the problem of the determination of the appropriate compensation to be paid to losers in integration schemes in which inefficient industries are established.[51] Thus he postulated that in an economic union between two countries, A and B, in which an industry is established in A, A should compensate B for the difference in the price charged by A and the world price times the quantity consumed by B. Mead argues that this is the appropriate compensation by saying:

In a sense, then, we have rehabilitated our rule of thumb as a sound and fair minimum compensation principle, not because we know that in every case it provides a measure of A's gain at B's expense, but in the sense that it continues to give a measure of B's losses. A's gains may or may not be larger than this; it is up to A to evaluate these gains, then to decide whether the gains are large enough to pay the compensation. If not, A should choose the option of not establishing the industry.[52]

The second instrument available for improving the distribution of benefits from integration is a development bank. Such an institution could influence the distribution of the benefits by extending low cost loans to the relatively less developed countries to enable the latter to improve their infrastructure and thus attract more industry. Alternately, the bank could lend its funds directly to those industries locating in the relatively less developed countries and thus increase the attractiveness of locating in those countries. The disadvantage of such a system is that the bank may be forced to lend funds for economically unsound projects if minimum limits are set on the proportion of the bank's funds that have to be lent to the relatively less developed countries. Further, even the relatively more developed of the LDCs entering into integration schemes cannot contribute large amounts of capital to such banks and therefore the impact of such banks' policies on the distribution of benefits may be rather limited.[53]

Another type of regional institution, similar to the development bank because of its international character, is the regional international company suggested by I.M.D. Little in his article "Regional International Companies as an Approach to Economic Integration."[54] Little suggested that, when industries could only be reasonably established on a regional basis, these industries should be established as regional international companies. Such companies would be jointly owned by the member countries and would distribute profits according to the shares owned by the various countries. The problems of the location of such industries could be mitigated by requiring the host countries to provide tax-free status to these industries and to compensate them for any benefits to be derived from them. The principal problems confronting the establishment of these companies appears to be the estimation of the compensation to be paid by the host countries, the determination of the control of the companies, and the rates of participation of the various countries.

The third instrument for alleviating inequities in the distribution of benefits of the list presented above is the granting of options for the retainment of tariffs. The relatively less developed countries are permitted to either retain some of their tariffs or to reduce them at a slower rate than their more developed partners. The disadvantage of this provision, which is designed to enable the relatively less developed countries to protect their domestic industries, is that it may also limit the benefits from integration: it is possible that the potential trade promising the greatest benefits may be thwarted.

The distribution of the benefits of integration can also be improved by means of complementation agreements. The objective of such agreements is to provide for coordinated industrialization in the various countries by assigning industries or stages of industries to the various countries. Given the general interest in industrialization in LDCs, complementation agreements appear to be a suitable tool for the improvement of the distribution of the benefits resulting from integration. However, as determined by the experiences of CACM, LAFTA, and UDEAC, such agreements are very difficult to negotiate in practice. Complementation agreements are very difficult to negotiate because industries are assigned one at a time among the various member countries and thus provide for only one beneficiary at a time.

The problem of assigning only one industry at a time can best be circumvented by allocating "packages" of industries as suggested by Balassa and Stoutjesdijk.[55] The advantage of allocating "packages" of industries is that all countries are assigned at least one industry. However, discounting this advantage, these industry allocation arrangements are also very difficult to negotiate as revealed by the experience of the Andean Common Market described in the last chapter. The next section of this chapter is devoted to an analysis of the proposals that have been made for economically allocating the industries of such "packages" among the member countries.

II

The location of industries in integration schemes among less developed countries can be determined by inter-country negotiations or through the use of comprehensive economic models. Both of these approaches are, however, generally hampered by the lack of adequate data. This lack of data makes negotiations uncertain and therefore difficult and precludes the calculation of the costs and the benefits of particular locations required by planning models.

The allocation of industry by means of intergovernmental bargaining has the advantage that it requires little data and that it should hopefully not require too much time. However, the advantages are also the main disadvantages. Decisions that are made without the appropriate data also imply that the negotiated solution may not be optimal and that actually some members may end up worse off than if allocation had been determined by the market. Further, the lack of data also produces great uncertainty and negotiations may stagnate rather than produce timely results.

Planning models have not yet been utilized to allocate industries in less developed countries, as indicated by Morawetz who stated that "No integration scheme among developing countries has used a comprehensive economic model to allocate new industries among member countries."[56] Nevertheless a number of theoretical models have been formulated to accomplish this objective. Foremost among the models that have been proposed is that by Schydlowsky,[57] which "is attractive because it solves the whole industrial location problem efficiently and equitably in one fell swoop."[58] However, the model's principal disadvantage in practice "is that the data requirements of the model are prohibitive."[59]

Schydlowsky developed a comprehensive linear programming model to allocate industry in the Andean Common Market. The model is one of maximization subject to distributional constraints. He defined the benefits as the difference between the net foreign exchange saved and the real foreign exchange value of the factors of production employed. The net foreign exchange saved would be given by the difference between the gross foreign exchange saved and the value of the internationally traded inputs that entered into the production of the import substitute. The real foreign exchange value of the factors of production would be obtained by valuing these factors at their social marginal cost and converting this sum at the marginal utility of foreign exchange. Schydlowsky suggested two distributional constraints: equal per capita benefit to each of the participating countries and equal weighted by per capita income benefit to each of the countries.

The proposed approach is appealing because it efficiently solves the problem of allocating industry in an equitable manner. In practice, however, it cannot be implemented because the "difficulty confronting the methodology outlined . . . arises from the lack of project data. Indeed, without fairly complete project information on each of the integration industries (or projects) a calculation of the kind described is impossible."[60]

A program such as Schydlowsky's could only be implemented if data such as that available to Martin Carnoy[61] were available for all integration industries in all the member countries. Carnoy designed a study to determine the least cost location of six industry groups in the Latin American Free Trade Association. Although the study did not develop a dynamic framework, it extended the traditional static analysis to allow for different sized plants and economies of scale. The stated limitations of the model developed by Carnoy, however, suggest the impossibility of implementing it to allocate industry in the Andean Common Market. The study is restricted to the allocation of six industries, chosen mainly on the basis of data considerations, and to those countries whose economic institutes furnished cost studies.

The model developed is one that minimizes the sum of the costs of production and transportation of the final product inputs and the costs of production and transportation of the final product. The objective function of this linear programming model is constrained by both technological and market restrictions. The model allocates industries or parts of industries to the countries on the basis of absolute cost advantages since there are no capacity or distributional constraints.

However, even for a limited study such as Carnoy's, the data problems and the limited reliability of estimates are of considerable importance. In the Carnoy study each of the economic institutes in each of the countries was asked to furnish projections of future demand for two given time periods and to provide estimates of the transportation and production costs. As stated by Carnoy, the estimates of future demand and transportation costs provided by the economic institutes could be accepted as being relatively consistent. Carnoy, however, discovered that the estimates of production costs were less reliable and presented greater problems because the economic institutes envisioned different sized plants, did not consistently estimate either short-run or long-run costs, and differed in their estimations according to whether they based their cost studies on already existing plants or on shadow prices. Given the estimation problems mentioned by Carnoy and recognizing the usual problems in shadow price determination it can be concluded that in practice the study only approximated the minimum cost solution.

Therefore the model formulated by Carnoy suffers from the same limitations as the Schydlowsky model in allocating integration industries in the Andean Common Market. Both models impose impossible data requirements and their implementation is consequently impractical.

In a more recent paper Baanante and Simmons[62] utilized an approach very similar to that of Carnoy to determine the optimal amounts of nitrogenous fertilizers to be produced in each of the Andean Common Market countries. They formulated a linear programming model to minimize an objective function representing the sum of the production and transportation costs of the input, ammonia, and the costs of production and transportation of the final products—urea, ammonium nitrate compounds, and Chilean nitrates. The final outputs were, however, not treated separately but rather were lumped together as one final output.

In their study Baanante and Simmons confronted the same problems as Carnoy: the determination of the costs of production. Baanante and Simmons determined the costs of production from the production coefficients determined by the Tennessee Valley Authority in feasibility studies in some Andean countries and the costs of both fixed and variable inputs. In general they assumed that the initial investment costs and the costs of all the relatively fixed inputs such as labor, laboratory costs, and maintenance were equal in all countries. They did, however, determine the market value costs for variable inputs such as raw materials and electrical power. The study by Baanante and Simmons underlines the conclusion that the approach developed by Carnoy would not be appropriate for the allocation of a large number of industries in the Andean Common Market because the data requirements would be excessive.

David Kendrick[63] proposed the staggering of investment projects over time and space as a solution to the problem of allocating industries in economic integration schemes and formulated a mixed integer programming model to accomplish this. The model was designed to minimize the sum of the costs of production of the final goods and the costs of transportation of both inputs and the final product over several time periods subject to capacity, market, and indivisibility constraints. However, robbed of its refinements the model is similar to that of Carnoy and therefore is also impractical because of the insurmountable data requirements.

Without concerning himself directly with the allocation of industry within a common market, Dermont Gately[64] analyzed the problem of the distribution of benefits. Gately suggested a game theoretic framework to determine which distributions of benefits would be acceptable to induce countries to join the union. He defined the benefits from participation as the sum of the production and the consumption effects. The production benefits for a given industry in a given country would be given by the value of the increased output made possible by the larger market less the shadow costs of the factors employed in producing the extra output. The consumption effects would be determined by the changes in consumer surplus and government revenue. Then, assuming that the benefits to all the countries from different industrial allocations could be calculated, the distribution acceptable to all could be analyzed in a game theoretic context. Gately's model does not produce an optimum solution but still presents the obvious problem of impossible data requirements.

Thus, it can be concluded that the practical problem of actually allocating industries in integration schemes among less developed countries has not been solved. The optimization models presented in the literature impose such impossible data requirements that they do not aid the member countries in assigning industries in better ways than pure negotiation. Therefore, in the next chapter a model will be formulated that will not be subject to such stringent data requirements and that can therefore provide some indication in practice as to how to allocate industries in integration schemes among LDCs and in the Andean Common Market in particular.

3 THE THEORETICAL MODEL DESIGNED FOR THE PRACTICAL ALLOCATION OF INDUSTRIES

The problem of allocating the industries of the Sectorial Programs of Industrial Development in the Andean Common Market is a problem of considerable magnitude. It is a difficult task because of the large number of industries included in each of the programs and because of the lack of adequate data to judge the future efficiency of each of those industries in each of the member countries. The problem is the development of a method that will, subject to distributional constraints, assign the various industries to the member countries so as to minimize the total cost of supplying the region with the products of the industries included in these programs. The distributional constraints are designed to assure that all the countries are assigned at least some industries and that the industries are allocated in a manner acceptable to all countries.

The Andean Common Market is, contrary to the implications of its name, not a common market. It can best be defined as a free trade area where the member countries retain the prerogative to impose certain trade restrictions on intrazonal trade for the purpose of protecting their national industries. Although the member countries agreed on a minimum common external tariff they have not been able to agree upon a common external tariff and such an agreement does furthermore not seem likely in the near future. The elimination of intra-area trade restrictions also appears to be a goal that could easily be postponed indefinitely. The objective therefore is the formulation of a method to allocate industries within a free trade area in which the products of the assigned industries, but not their inputs, are freely traded.

In this chapter, therefore, some generally accepted investment criteria designed for the single-country case will first be discussed. Next, from these criteria a criterion for allocating industries in a multi-country situation, the domestic resource cost (DRC) criterion, is selected and an objective function is formulated for a mixed integer programming model designed to minimize the costs of supplying the regional demands for the products from the assignable industries. However, the calculation of DRCs imposes great data requirements. Therefore the relation between the domestic resource cost and the effective rate of protection (ERP) is introduced. Since the former measure can be estimated from the latter, certain data problems are circumvented.

The objective function estimable from effective rates of protection is then expanded by the addition of the transport costs of the final goods. These costs are included in the objective function because of their possible effect on the comparative advantage of a particular country when called to supply the whole area.

Having established an objective function, it is next necessary to establish a set of distributional constraints. A number of possible distributional constraints are formulated. Lastly, some of the limitations of the suggested approach are examined. However, it is pointed out that in spite of the possible criticism the model provides a useful tool for analyzing industrial allocation in practice.

I

The problem of allocating a number of industries among countries is similar to the problem of allocating scarce funds among projects. The latter is a one-country problem that has been extensively studied and for which a set of investment criteria has been developed. An appropriate question is whether any of these criteria is also applicable to the multi-country assignment problem.

A number of investment criteria have been proposed in the literature. However, these criteria all have as a common denominator the requirement that projects be evaluated on the basis of net social benefit, given by the difference between real social benefits and real opportunity costs. Furthermore, three of these criteria—the social marginal productivity criterion, the rate of return to capital criterion, and the domestic resource cost criterion—are equivalent in theory provided that the correct shadow prices are employed.

The social marginal productivity criterion requires that the net benefits of a project be positive. The net benefits of a project at the margin can easily be computed if the shadow prices for resources, inputs, and outputs are given. Such shadow prices could conceivably be derived from a full, general equilibrium inter-temporal optimizing model. Any project i can be represented by $G + J$ coefficients, where G are input and output coefficients in terms of domestically produced commodities and J are factor input and output and imported commodity input coefficients. Given these coefficients and the shadow prices for inputs and outputs, the benefits per unit of a project i can be calculated from the following equation:

$$B = \sum_{g=1}^{G} a_{gi} P_g - \sum_{j=1}^{J} v_{ji} s_j \qquad (1)$$

B = net benefit of a project i.

a_{gi} = physical input (if negative) and output (if positive) coefficients for domestic goods.

P_g = shadow prices for domestic goods.

v_{ji} = physical input and output coefficients for factors and imported inputs.

s_j = shadow prices for factors and imported inputs.

The social marginal productivity criterion requires that B be greater than zero for the acceptance of a project. This criterion, if evaluated with shadow prices derived from a general equilibrium model, is logically equivalent to the criterion based on the rate of return to capital. This can be demonstrated by letting capital be the Jth factor input with a unit shadow price of K and a shadow rate of return r in equation 1. Setting B equal to zero and rearranging, it is possible to write:

$$r = \frac{\displaystyle\sum_{g=1}^{G} a_{gi} P_g - \sum_{j=1}^{J-1} v_{ij} s_j}{v_{Ji} K} \qquad (2)$$

(Notation for equations 2 through 4 is the same as that for equation 1.)

The requirement that B be greater than zero set by the social marginal productivity criterion is equivalent to the requirement that the rate of return to capital for a project, r, be larger than the shadow rate of return given by the general equilibrium model. In a similar way Bruno and Krueger developed the criterion of domestic resource cost of a unit of foreign exchange earned or saved by defining foreign exchange as a factor of production. Thus, if the first factor of production is foreign exchange, equation **1** can be written as:

$$B = \sum_{g=1}^{G} a_{gi} P_g + v_{1i} s_1 - \sum_{j=2}^{J} v_{ji} s_j \tag{3}$$

where v_{1i} represents the net amount of foreign exchange earned or saved due to the project. It is given by the difference between the marginal foreign exchange revenue, u_i, and the marginal import requirements, m_i, caused by the project. Rearranging equation **3**, the domestic resource cost of an activity is given by:

$$s_1 = \frac{\sum_{j=2}^{J} v_{ji} s_j - \sum_{g=1}^{G} a_{gi} P_g}{(u_i - m_i)} \tag{4}$$

The domestic resource cost criterion therefore ranks projects according to the domestic resource cost of earning or saving a unit of foreign exchange. That is, this criterion ranks projects according to the cost of resources, domestic value added, necessary for the production of a unit of international value added.[1] Projects are accepted if the DRC measure is less than the shadow rate of exchange derived from a general equilibrium model and rejected otherwise.

Thus in theory in a one-country situation the social marginal productivity, the rate of return to capital, and the domestic resource cost criteria are identical. A project for which the benefits are positive, as calculated with the first criterion, will present an effective rate of return to capital greater than the shadow rate of return, as required by the second criterion, and will yield a domestic resource cost measure smaller than the shadow exchange rate, as established by the third criterion. In practice, however, for the allocation of industries among countries in a free trade area only the social marginal productivity criterion can be used. The rate of return to capital and the DRC criteria cannot be employed because the utilization of these criteria implies the comparison of the rate of return to capital and of the domestic resource cost with the shadow rate of return to capital and the shadow exchange rate. These shadow rates are different in the different countries.

The criterion developed by Bruno and Krueger can, however, be utilized to assign industries in a multi-country situation if the DRCs computed for the various industries in the different countries are divided by the shadow exchange rates in the various countries. Dividing the DRCs by the shadow exchange rates has the effect of standardizing the DRCs to the same units: dollars of cost of domestic resources per dollars of international value added cancel and leave the DRCs as pure numbers. The criterion for assigning industries given standardized DRCs, referred to simply as DRCs, corresponds exactly with the social marginal productivity criterion. The social marginal productivity criterion assigns industries to the countries that demonstrate the largest difference between the international value added gained and the domestic cost of resources divided by the value of the shadow exchange rate. The DRC criterion assigns industries to the countries demonstrating the lowest ratio between the measure of the domestic cost of resources divided by the shadow exchange rate and the measure of international value added. Furthermore, the DRC criterion presented coincides with the Corden measure of effective protection as will be demonstrated in Section IV. Because it is an appropriate criterion for industry allocation and because it corresponds to the Corden effective rate of protection measure, the DRC criterion is selected as the basis for the formulation of the objective function of an integer program designed to allocate industries in a free trade area.

II

In order to minimize the cost of supplying the area with the products of a given set of industries in the absence of distributional constraints it would suffice to assign the industries to the countries demonstrating the lowest DRCs for those industries. The objective function of an integer programming model designed to allocate the given industries given no distributional constraints would be written as:

$$\text{Minimize } R = \sum_{k} \sum_{i} x_i^k Z_i^k \tag{5}$$

where x_i^k stands for the domestic resource cost of a unit of international value added in industry i in country k and Z_i^k is a dichotomous variable that assumes the values of one and zero depending on whether industry i is assigned to country k or not.

However, given distributional constraints, in order to minimize the costs of supplying the area it is necessary to consider the relative sizes of the industries in terms of their total international value added because the assignment of industries on the basis of pure DRCs could lead to higher cost solutions. Therefore, in the formulation of an objective function for an integer allocation program each of the DRCs for the various industries in the various countries is weighted by the ratio of the total international value added in the industry to the sum of the total international values added in all industries. The total international value added in one industry is defined as the product of the international value added in the production of one unit and the number of units required. Thus, the objective function of an integer program designed to allocate industries subject to constraints is formulated as:

$$\text{Minimize} \quad \sum_k \sum_i x_i^k \frac{W_i}{W_T} Z_i^k \qquad (6)$$

where:

x_i^k = stands for the domestic resource cost of producing one unit of good i in country k.

W_i = total international value added in industry i.

W_T = total international value added in all industries to be assigned.

Z_i^k = dichotomous variable taking on the value of one or zero depending on whether industry i is assigned to country k or not.

III

In order to utilize the concept of DRC to allocate industries in a free trade area it is necessary to express equation **4** in more detail. To do this we assume that the industries to be allocated will have no home good outputs and that the home good inputs do not have an imported component, where home goods are defined as goods that are not traded because of their relatively high transport costs. Then the G coefficients will reflect home inputs and if we change our convention and denote inputs by positive coefficients then the numerator of the DRC equation will stand for the sum of the domestic factor inputs and the home good inputs. Further, assuming only one output with an international price P_i and letting the marginal import requirements in country k for industry i be given by the sum of $g = G_i^k + 1, \ldots, H$ imported input coefficients times their prices, equation **4** can be rewritten as:

$$x_i^k = \frac{\left(\sum_{j=2}^{J} v_{ji} s_j + \sum_{g=1}^{G_i^k} a_{gi} P_g \right) f}{P_i - \sum_{g=G_i^k+1}^{H_i} a_{gi} P_g} \qquad (7)$$

where:

x_i^k = stands for s_1, the domestic resource cost of producing one unit of international value added in good i in country k.

v_{ji} = physical factor input coefficients.

a_{gi} = physical input good coefficients.

s_j = shadow price of factor j.

P_g = shadow prices of home inputs $g = 1, \ldots, G$ and international prices for inputs $g = G_i^k + 1, \ldots, H$.

P_i = international price of good i.

f = reciprocal of economy-wide shadow exchange rate.

$g = 1, \ldots, G_i^k$ = domestic goods utilized in the production of good i in country k.

$g = G_i^k + 1, \ldots, H_i$ = imported goods utilized in the production of good i in country k.

The second numerator term of equation 7 represents the indirect value added by the domestic factors through the utilization of home good inputs. Because the value of the home goods is equal to the sum of the costs of the inputs used in their production, the second numerator term can be expressed in terms of the input coefficients for home goods, the factor inputs utilized in the production of home goods, and the shadow prices of the factors of production and equation 7 can be rewritten as:

$$x_i^k = \frac{\left(\sum_{j=2}^{J} v_{ji} s_j + \sum_{g=1}^{G_i^k} \sum_{j=2}^{J} a_{gi} v_{jg} s_j \right) f}{P_i - \sum_{g=G_i^k+1}^{H_i} a_{gi} P_g} \tag{8}$$

(Notation for equation 8 is the same as that for equation 7.)

IV

The calculation of the domestic resource costs for the objective function given by equation 6 would however be a nearly impossible task if equation 8 were used as the measure of domestic resource cost. DRCs cannot practically be computed for a large number of industries in several countries. The problems result from the lack of adequate shadow prices for the factors of production in the various countries and the absence of minutely detailed input-output data for the industries and particularly for their domestically produced inputs.

Because of the impossibility of calculating DRCs by the use of equation 8 it is necessary to resort to the nearly identical measure, the effective rate of protection. Given a unit official foreign exchange rate, the effective rate of protection is equivalent to the DRC but for the addition of one to the ERP. The ERP measure establishes the value added by the factors of production as the difference between the prices of the final goods and the prices of inputs in much the same way that in national income accounting gross national product can be estimated from the prices of goods rather than from the returns to the factors of production.

In the literature, however, there has been a great deal of controversy on the equivalence of the two measures and the conditions for their identity. The controversy about the equivalence of DRC and ERP has resulted mainly because of the existence of two methods for calculating ERP, the Corden and the Balassa methods, which deal differently with home goods. This controversy has further led to a discussion as to whether the efficiency of an activity should be judged as a whole, including home inputs, or whether the latter should be excluded. The other elements presented that would lead to the nonequivalence of the DRC and ERP measures in a given country are the existence of foreign factors of production and the violation of either the domestic perfect competition or existence of optimal tariffs assumptions.

Krueger states that the DRC and ERP measures are identical only if the following conditions are met: "(1) all goods are traded (or tradable); (2) there are no transportation costs; (3) factors of production are perfectly mobile within the domestic economy but perfectly immobile internationally; and (4) all domestic markets are perfectly competitive."[2] The first of Krueger's assumptions is redundant according to Balassa and Schydlowsky[3] because in the absence of transportation costs all goods are tradable. More important, Balassa and Schydlowsky add the assumption that the country use an optimal set of tariffs and export taxes to equate the domestic product prices to marginal revenue from import substituting and exporting. Therefore, given Balassa and Schydlowsky's assumption and that Krueger's third and fourth assumptions hold, the issue is whether the DRC and the ERP measures are equivalent if transportation costs are not zero and consequently there are nontraded goods.

Krueger stated that the DRC and ERP measures would be different if there were home goods. This would indeed be the case if the ERP were computed using the Balassa method. This ERP measure is given by the ratio of the difference between only the direct domestic and international values added to the direct international values added. Thus with the Balassa method the domestic value added is given by the difference between the domestic price of output and the domestic value of all inputs, both tradable and home goods. The domestic value of the home goods is given by the sum of the domestic value of the tradable inputs that enter into the production of nontraded goods and the value of the pure home goods and of the primary factors that are utilized in the production of these goods. The international value added is obtained by subtracting the value of home goods, valued at international prices, from the difference between the international price of output and the value of the sum of tradable inputs valued at international prices.

The Corden method differs from the Balassa method in that in the former the domestic value of the nontraded goods that enter as inputs to the production activity is included in the total domestic value added measure of the activity. That is, the Corden method uses a total rather than a direct measure of domestic value added. Similarly the measure of international value added includes the international value of the domestic resources employed in the production of the nontraded inputs. The ERP measure computed by using the Corden method will be equivalent to the DRC, given that there are no foreign factors of production, that markets are in perfect competition, and that tariffs and export taxes are optimal. Thus the domestic resource cost measure given by equation 8 can also be written as:[4]

$$
x_i^k = \frac{P_i(1 + t_i^k) - \sum_{g=1}^{H_i} a_{gi} P_g (1 + t_g^k) + \sum_{g=1}^{G_i^k} a_{gi} P_g (1 + t_g^k)}{P_i - \sum_{g=1}^{H_i} a_{gi} P_g + \sum_{g=1}^{G_i^k} a_{gi} P_g} \tag{9}
$$

where:

$g = 1, \ldots, H_i$ = all inputs into i.

$g = 1, \ldots, G_i^k$ = domestic inputs into i in country k.

x_i^k = domestic resource cost of a unit of foreign exchange earned in industry i in country k.

P_i = international price of good i.

t_i^k = tariff on good i in country k.

a_{gi} = physical input coefficient.

The first two terms in the numerator of equation 7 represent the direct value added by the domestic factors of production and are equivalent to the first term of equation 8. The third term in 9 is the same as the second in 8 and represents the indirect value added by the domestic factors through the production of home inputs for industry i. The denominator in **9** represents the total value added by the domestic factors valued at international prices.

Further complications arise if import tariffs and export taxes are allowed to be nonoptimal. Like transport costs, tariffs make possible the domestic production of inputs that would otherwise be imported. Again there are differences between the Balassa and Corden methods of estimating the effective protective rate and again it is obvious that the DRC concept is equivalent to the Corden ERP concept.

Given transport costs and nonoptimal tariffs and export taxes the issue whether DRC is equivalent to Corden's ERP or Balassa's ERP raises the further question as to which of the two ERP measures is the appropriate investment criterion. As pointed out by Balassa and Schydlowsky if there were no transport costs and nonoptimal tariffs and taxes there would be no home goods and it would not matter whether we evaluate the project on the basis of processing costs in the last stage of fabrication or combine costs at all stages.[5] If the given conditions are not met, however, the direct and total measures of domestic resource cost will not be equal. This situation results from the fact that the market prices for goods and factors will no longer equal the shadow prices. Thus in the evaluation of projects, those with high priced inputs will be discriminated against if a total rather than a direct domestic resource cost measure is taken. Balassa argues that this measure of ERP, which measures only direct domestic resource cost at the last stage of fabrication, should be the appropriate project selection criterion because it does not penalize projects due to the high priced inputs that are possible as a result of transport costs and nonoptimal tariffs. However, he notes that the total domestic resource cost measure, proposed by Bruno and Krueger and equivalent to Corden's ERP, is superior if: "(a) all existing industries will be maintained, (b) the expansion of the output of any one industry will bring forth increased output of all domestic industries providing direct and indirect inputs into it (i.e., the direct and indirect marginal input coefficients of domestic resources and of imports taken to equal the corresponding average coefficients), and (c) costs in input producing industries will continue at existing levels."[6] Since it is apparent that changes in the domestic demands will be satisfied by domestic firms, it appears that the Corden measure of ERP would be the more appropriate.[7]

If nonoptimal tariffs and export taxes are applied, the market prices of the domestic factors of production will no longer equal their opportunity costs or shadow prices. Balassa and Schydlowsky point out that in a situation with nonoptimal tariffs and taxes, "shadow prices will reflect neither the marginal social cost of inputs into the project nor the marginal social utility of its output."[8] Therefore, the DRC calculated from shadow prices for factors of production, equation 8, will no longer be equivalent to the DRC calculated from the prices of goods as given in equation 9.

Ideally, "in making decisions on projects, one should therefore use second-best shadow prices reflecting marginal social costs and utilities under existing policies, with adjustment made for prospective policy changes."[9] These second-best shadow prices should be derived from a full general equilibrium system incorporating the present policies. Again, the acquisition of such shadow prices would be very difficult.

Because of the complications in practice in finding shadow prices, Balassa and Schydlowsky suggest that projects be ranked by DRCs evaluated at market prices. The DRC can be computed from market prices for the primary factors of production by using equation 8. This computation would be feasible for only a very limited number of projects in any country because of the difficulties of getting data, prices as well as coefficients, for detailed activities where the primary factors could be subdivided and reclassified into any number of specialized sub-groups. Therefore, in practice it is preferable to calculate the DRCs for a large number of industries in several countries using the approximate market prices for goods given by the international prices plus the respective tariffs. That domestic prices do indeed reflect international prices plus tariffs is not only a firmly held principle in theory but is also suggested, at least for relatively basic homogeneous goods, by N.R. Norman's study of domestic price responses to changing tariffs in Britain.[10]

The Corden measure of effective protection and the resulting DRC obtained by adding one to the ERP can be altered so as to allow for international movements of factors. In order to do this, it is best to start by rewriting equation 8 as a benefit equation like equation 1.

$$B_i^k = \left(P_i - \sum_{g=G_i^k+1}^{H_i} a_{gi}P_g\right)x_i^k - \left(\sum_{j=2}^{J} v_{ji}s_j - \sum_{g=1}^{G_i^k}\sum_{j=2}^{J} a_{gi}v_{jg}s_j\right)f \quad (10)$$

where:

B_i^k = net benefit from the production of one unit of i in country k.

P_i = international price of good i.

a_{gi} = physical input coefficients establishing the amount of input g necessary for one unit of output i.

P_g = international prices for inputs $g = G_i^k+1, \ldots, H_i$.

x_i^k = here it stands for the cost of foreign exchange in industry i in country k.[11]

v_{ji} = amount of factor j necessary for the production of one unit of i in physical units.

s_j = shadow price of factor j.

v_{jg} = amount of factor j necessary for the production of input good g in physical units.

f = reciprocal of economy wide shadow exchange rate.

$g = 1, \ldots, G_i^k$ = domestic goods utilized in the production of good i in country k.

$g = G_i^k + 1, \ldots, H_i$ = imported goods utilized in the production of good i in country k.

Domestic capital can be treated like any other local factor of production and need not be separated from the other factors of production. Imported capital, factor J, will have a domestic price of Kx_i^k, where K is the international price of capital and x_i^k is the cost of foreign exchange in industry i in country k. Assuming for the time being that imported capital is not used in the production of home good inputs, and given a rate of return to capital in country k of r^k, equation **10** may be rewritten as:

$$B = \left(P_i - \sum_{g=G_i^k+1}^{H_i} a_{gi} P_g \right) x_i^k - \sum_{j=2}^{J-1} v_{ji} s_j f - v_{Ji} K r^k x_i^k$$

$$- \sum_{g=1}^{G_i} \sum_{j=2}^{J} a_{gi} v_{jg} s_j f - \sum_{g=1}^{G_i^k} a_{gi} v_{Jg} K r^k x_i^k \tag{11}$$

(Notation for equation **11** is the same as that for equation **10**.)

The third term of equation **11** represents the direct contribution to value added attributable to imported capital. This term can be interpreted to represent the rental payments to imported capital.

Assuming that no foreign factors are employed in the production of home goods, the set of factors of production can be redefined to allow for foreign ownership of factors of production. Thus the foreign owned factors and their direct contributions to value added can be separated into a one-factor category, $J=2$. If the repatriated return to factor $J=2$ in country k is s_2^k and the shadow rate of exchange is x_i^k, equation **11** can be written as:

$$B = \left(P_i - \sum_{g=G_i^k+1}^{H_i} a_{gi} P_g \right) x_i^k - \sum_{J=3}^{J-1} v_{ji} s_j f - v_{Ji} K r^k x_i^k$$

$$- v_{2i} s_2^k x_i^k - \sum_{g=1}^{G_i^k} \sum_{J=2}^{J} a_{gi} v_{jg} s_j f \tag{12}$$

(Notation for equation 12 is the same as that for equation 13.)

Setting B equal to zero in equation 12 and rearranging the domestic resource cost of a unit of foreign exchange saved or earned can be obtained as:

$$x_i^k = \frac{\left(\sum_{j=3}^{J-1} v_{ji} s_j + \sum_{g=1}^{G_i^k} \sum_{j=2}^{J} a_{gi} v_{jg} s_j \right) f}{P_i - \sum_{g=G_i^k+1}^{H_i} a_{gi} P_g - v_{Ji} Kr^k - v_{2i} s_2^k} \tag{13}$$

where:

x_i^k = the domestic resource cost of a unit of foreign exchange saved or earned.

v_{ji} = the amount of factor j necessary for the production of one unit of good i in physical units.

s_j = the shadow price of factor j.

a_{gi} = the amount of input g necessary for the production of one unit of good i in physical units.

v_{jg} = the amount of factor j necessary for the production of input good g.

P_i = international price of good i.

P_g = international price of good g.

v_{Ji} = amount of imported capital necessary for the production of one unit of i.

K = international price of capital.

r^k = rate of return to capital in country k.

v_{2i} = amount of factor 2, foreign factors, employed in the production of good i.

s_2^k = repatriated return to foreign factors of production in country k.

f = reciprocal of economy wide shadow exchange rate.

$g = 1, \ldots, G_i^k$ = domestic goods utilized in the production of good i in country k.

$g = G_i^k + 1, \ldots, H_i$ = imported goods utilized in the production of good i in country k.

Thus in order to allow for imported and foreign owned factors of production their contributions to value added were subtracted from both the numerator and denominator of the original expression for DRC presented in equation 8. Making these corrections to equation 8, where the domestic value added was calculated from domestic output prices, the DRC can be expressed as:

$$x_i^k = \frac{P_i(1 + t_i^k) - \displaystyle\sum_{g=G_i^k+1}^{H_i} a_{gi} P_g (1 + t_g^k) - v_{Ji} Kr^k - v_{2i} s_2^k}{P_i - \displaystyle\sum_{g=G_i^k+1}^{H_i} a_{gi} P_g - v_{Ji} Kr^k - v_{2i} s_2^k} \tag{14}$$

where:

t_i^k = tariff on good i in country k.
t_g^k = tariff on input good g in country k.

(Other notation is the same as that of equation **13**.)

In order to simplify the derivation of equation **14**, two assumptions were made. First, it was assumed that no tradable inputs were used in the production of home good inputs. Second, it was assumed that imported capital and foreign factors of production were not utilized in the production of the home goods utilized as inputs to the production of the final good i. These two assumptions, which were employed to simplify the derivation of equation **14**, will now be relaxed by adjusting both the numerator and denominator of equation **14** for the contributions to value added attributable to tradable inputs, imported capital, and foreign factors of production.

In order to simplify the derivation of the expression for the indirect contribution to value added attributable to tradable inputs through the various stages of production of home goods leading to the production of the final good inputs, the adjustments for imported capital and foreign factors of production will be ignored. That is, it will be assumed that given no imported inputs into the production of home goods, the indirect value added by the domestic factors through the production of home goods will be given simply like in equation **7** as:

$$N = \sum_{g=1}^{G_i^k} a_{gi} P_g^* \tag{15}$$

where:

N = indirect value added by the domestic factors through the production of home goods.

a_{gi} = the amount of input g necessary for the production of one unit of i in physical units.

P_g^* = domestic price of good g equals international price plus tariff, P_g^* = $P_g (1 + t_g^k)$.

$g = 1 \ldots G_i^k$ = domestic goods utilized in the production of good i in country k.

Allowing for tradable inputs in the final stage of production of home goods, the value added by the domestic factors is given by:

$$N = \sum_{g=1}^{G_i^k} a_{gi} \left[P_g^* - \sum_{s_1 = s_1^k + 1}^{S_1} Q_{s_1g}^1 \, P_{s_1} \, (1 + t_{s_1}^k) \right] \tag{16}$$

where:

$Q_{s_1g}^1$ = the amount of input s_1 necessary for the production of one unit of good g in physical units.

P_{s_1} = international price of good s_1.

$t_{s_1}^k$ = tariff on good s_1 in country k.

$s_1 = s_1^k + 1, \ldots, S_1$ = tradable inputs utilized in the production of good g in country k.

In the term in brackets in equation **16**, the value of the tradable inputs used is subtracted from the value of the home good g. Next, it is assumed that either the value of the factors employed in the production of home good g is zero or that it can be included as a home good so that the value of home good g is equal to the sum of the value added contributions of the home good inputs and of the imported inputs utilized in the production of g. This assumption is employed only to simplify the presentation and does not have any effect on the expression of the indirect contribution of inputs that is going to be derived, since this expression will be formulated as the amount that will have to be subtracted from the numerator and denominator of equation **14**. Given the aforementioned assumption it is possible to write:

$$\sum_{s_1 = 1}^{s_1} Q_{s_1g}^1 P_{s_1}^* = P_g^* - \sum_{s_1 = s_1 + 1}^{S_1} Q_{s_1g}^1 P_{s_1} \, (1 + t_{s_1}^k) \tag{17}$$

where:

$Q_{s_1g}^1$ = the amount of input s_1 necessary for the production of one unit of good g in physical units.

$P^*_{s_1}$ = domestic price of good s_1.

P^*_g = domestic price of good g.

P_{s_1} = international price of good s_1.

$t^k_{s_1}$ = tariff on good s_1 in country k.

$s_1 = 1, \ldots, s_1$ = home good inputs.

$s_1 = s_1 + 1, \ldots, S_1$ = tradable inputs.

Equation **16** can now be rewritten as:

$$N = \sum_{g=1}^{G^k_i} a_{gi} \sum_{s_1=1}^{s_1} Q_{s_1 g} P^*_{s_1} \tag{18}$$

Next, it is assumed that tradable inputs were also used in the production of home goods $s_1 = 1 \ldots s_1$. Equation **18** is now rewritten as:

$$N = \sum_{g=1}^{G^k_i} a_{gi} \sum_{s_1=1}^{s_1} Q^1_{s_1 g} \left[P^*_{s_1} - \sum_{s_2=s_2+1}^{S_2} Q^2_{s_2 s_1} P_{s_2} (1 + t_{s_2}) \right] \tag{19}$$

where the new notation is:

$Q^2_{s_2 s_1}$ = the amount of input s_1 necessary for the production of one unit of good s_1 in physical units.

$s_2 = 1, \ldots, s_2$ = home good inputs utilized in the production of s_1.

$s_2 = s_2 + 1, \ldots, S_2$ = tradable inputs utilized in the production of s_1.

In equation **16** the value added assignable to tradable inputs employed in the production of home good g was eliminated. In equation **19** the value added contributed indirectly by tradable inputs through the production of the home good inputs $s_1 = 1, \ldots, s_1$ utilized in the production of home good g was eliminated. In the same manner it would be possible to continue backward and eliminate the value added contributed by tradable inputs in all stages of production of home goods.

Substituting equation **17** into **19** the following expression is obtained:

$$N = \sum_{g=1}^{G^k_i} a_{gi} \left[P^*_g - \sum_{s_1=s_1+1}^{S_1} Q^1_{s_1 g} P_{s_1} (1 + t^k_{s_1}) - \right.$$
$$\left. \sum_{s_1=1}^{s_1} \sum_{s_2=s_2+1}^{S_2} Q^2_{s_2 s_1} P_{s_2} (1 + t^k_{s_2}) \right] \tag{20}$$

From equation **20** it can be inductively determined that the value attributable to tradable inputs to be subtracted from the numerator of equation **14** is given by:

$$
Y^k_{in} = \sum_{g=1}^{G^k_i} \sum_{s_1=s_1+1}^{S_1} Q^1_{s_1 g} P_{s_1} (1 + t^k_{s_1})
$$

$$
+ \sum_{g=1}^{G^k_i} \sum_{s_1=1}^{S_1} \sum_{s_2=s_2+1}^{S_2} Q^2_{s_2 s_1} P_{s_2} (1 + t^k_{s_2})
$$

$$
+ \sum_{g=1}^{G^k_i} \sum_{s_1=1}^{S_1} \sum_{s_2=1}^{S_2} \sum_{s_3=s_3+1}^{S_3} Q^3_{s_3 s_2} P_{s_3} (1 + t^k_{s_3})
$$

$$
+ \quad \ldots
$$

$$
+ \sum_{g=1}^{G^k_i} \cdots \sum_{s_{t-1}=1}^{s_{t-1}} \sum_{s_t=s_t+1}^{S_t} Q^t_{s_t s_{t-1}} P_{s_t} (1 + t^k_{s_t}) \quad (21)
$$

where:

$1, \ldots, t$ = are the production stages of home goods.

Y^k_{in} = the value added contributed indirectly by tradable inputs utilized in all stages of home good production in country k. The subscript n refers to the fact that this value has to be subtracted from the numerator.

$Q^t_{s_t s_{t-1}}$ = the amount of input s_t utilized in the production of one unit of s_{t-1}.

P_{s_t} = international price of good s_t.

$t^k_{s_t}$ = tariff on good s_t in country k.

Equation **21** presents the value that has to be subtracted from the numerator because it was contributed by tradable inputs. A similar amount Y^k_{id} is subtracted from the denominator. The value Y^k_{id} is computed from equation **21** by setting all tariffs equal to zero.

Similarly the contributions to value added attributable to imported capital and foreign factors of production also have to be eliminated from both the numerator and denominator of equation **14**. The value contributed indirectly by imported capital through the production of the home goods utilized in the production of the final good is given by:

$$L_i^k = \sum_{g=1}^{G_i^k} a_{gi} \, v_{Jg} \, K r^k \tag{22}$$

where:

L_i^k = value added contributed by imported capital through the production of home goods.

a_{gi} = amount of input g necessary for the production of one unit of good i in physical units.

N_{Jg} = the amount of imported capital necessary for the production of input good g.

K = international price of capital.

r^k = rate of return to capital in country k.

Moving back to an earlier stage of production, the imported capital component of the home goods utilized for the production of home good g is given by:

$$\sum_{g=1}^{G_i^k} a_{gi} \sum_{s_1=1}^{s_1} Q_{s_1 g}^1 \, v_{Js_1} \, K r^k \tag{23}$$

where the new notation is:

$Q_{s_1 g}^1$ = the amount of input s_1 utilized for the production of good g.

v_{Js_1} = the amount of imported capital necessary for the production of input good s_1.

The value contributed by imported capital in the production of home goods in the two stages anterior to the production of the final good is given by adding the expression presented in equation 23 to equation 22. Given the sum of equations 22 and 23, inductively it can be determined that the value contributed by imported capital in all stages of home good production will be given by:

$$L_i^k = \sum_{g=1}^{G_i^k} a_{gi} \, v_{Jg} \, K r^k + \sum_{g=1}^{G_i^k} \sum_{s_1=1}^{s_1} a_{gi} \, Q_{s_1 g}^1 \, v_{Js_1} \, K r^k$$

$$+ \sum_{g=1}^{G_i^k} \sum_{s_1=1}^{s_1} \sum_{s_2=1}^{s_2} a_{gi} \, Q_{s_1 g}^1 \, Q_{s_2 s_1}^2 \, v_{Js_2} \, K r^k + \ldots$$

$$+ \sum_{g=1 \ldots s_{t-1}=1}^{G_i^k} \sum_{s_t=1}^{s_{t-1}} \sum_{s_t=1}^{s_t} a_{gi} \ldots Q_{s_t s_{t-1}}^t \, v_{Js_t} K \, r^k \tag{24}$$

where:

L_i^k = the value added contributed by imported capital through the production of home goods.

a_{gi} = the amount of input g necessary for the production of one unit of final good i in physical units.

$Q_{s_t}^t$ = the amount of input s_t necessary for the production of one unit of s_{t-1}.

v_{Js_t} = amount of imported capital necessary for the production of one unit of s_t.

K = international price of capital.

r^k = rate of return to capital in country k.

$g = 1, \ldots, G_i^k$ = home goods utilized in the production of good i in country k. The imported inputs are $g = G_i^k + 1 \ldots H_i$.

$s_t = 1, \ldots, s_t$ = home goods utilized in the production of good s_{t-1}. The imported inputs are $s_t = s_t + 1 \ldots S_t$.

The value contributed indirectly by imported capital through the production of home goods, L_i^k, is subtracted from both the numerator and denominator of equation 14. The indirect contribution attributable to foreign factors of production is given by an equation similar in form to that used to determine the contribution of imported capital:

$$F_i^k = \sum_{g=1}^{G_i^k} a_{gi} \, v_{2g} \, s_2^k + \sum_{g=1}^{G_i^k} \sum_{s_1=1}^{s_1} a_{gi} \, Q_{s_1 g}^1 \, v_{2s_1} \, s_2^k + , \ldots ,$$

$$+ \sum_{g=1}^{G_i^k} , \ldots , \sum_{s_{t-1}=1}^{s_{t-1}} \sum_{s_t=1}^{s_t} a_{gi}, \ldots , Q_{s_t s_{t-1}}^t \, v_{Js_t} \, s_2^k \tag{25}$$

where the notation is like that for equation 24 except for the following:

F_i^k = value added contributed by foreign factors of production through the production of home goods.

s_2^k = repatriated return to foreign factors of production in country k.

Allowing for the utilization of tradable inputs, imported capital, and foreign factors in the production of home goods, the domestic resource cost of foreign exchange is given as:

$$x_i^k = \frac{P_i(1 + t_i^k) - \sum_{g=G_i^k+1}^{H_i} a_{gi} P_g (1 + t_g^k) - N_{Ji} K r^l - N_{2i} s_2^k - Y_{in}^k - L_i^k - F_i^k}{P_i - \sum_{g=G_i^k+1}^{H_i} a_{gi} P_g - v_{Ji} K r^k - v_{2i} s_2^k - Y_{id}^k - L_i^k - F_i^k} \tag{26}$$

where:

x_i^k = the domestic resource cost of a unit of foreign exchange saved or earned.

a_{gi} = the amount of input g necessary for the production of one unit of good i in physical units.

P_i = international price of good i.

P_g = international price of good g.

v_{Ji} = amount of imported capital necessary for the production of one unit of i.

K = international price of capital.

r^k = rate of return to capital in country k.

v_{2i} = amount of factor 2 (foreign factors) employed in the production of good i.

s_2^k = repatriated return to foreign factors of production in country k.

Y_{in}^k = value added contributed by the tradable inputs valued at domestic prices utilized in the production of home goods in country k.

Y_{id}^k = value added contributed by the inputs valued at international prices utilized in the production of home goods in country k.

L_i^k = value added contributed by imported capital through the production of home goods.

F_i^k = value added contributed by foreign factors of production through the production of home goods.

$g = 1, \ldots, G_i^k$ = domestic goods utilized in the production of good i in country k.

$g = G_i^k + 1, \ldots, H_i$ = imported goods utilized in the production of good i in country k.

The last of Krueger's requirements for the equivalence of DRC and ERP+1 was that there was perfect competition in both factor and goods markets. The relaxation of this assumption obviously leads to the divergence between the shadow prices generated by a full general equilibrium system and the market prices. This provides a further reason to evaluate projects utilizing DRCs calculated from goods prices as ERP+1 rather than directly from market prices for factors of production because the latter cannot be traded and therefore their prices are likely to be more distorted.

V

In allocating industries among member countries in a free trade area it is also necessary to consider transport costs between producing and consuming countries. Therefore the transportation costs incurred in shipping goods from one country to other countries per unit of foreign exchange saved or earned have to be added to the DRC of each member country for each industry. Including transportion costs, the objective function (equation 6) can be rewritten as:

$$\text{Minimize } R = \sum_k \sum_i (x_i^k + c_i^k) \frac{W_i}{W_T} Z_i^k \tag{27}$$

where:

x_i^k = domestic resource cost of a unit of foreign exchange earned or saved in industry i in country k.

c_i^k = given an industry i assigned in a country k, the transport cost of satisfying the demands of countries $j \neq k$ per unit of foreign exchange earned or saved.

W_i = total international value added in industry i.

W_T = total international value in all industries to be assigned.

Z_i^k = is a dichotomous variable that assumes values of 0 and 1. It assumes the value 1 when an industry i is assigned to a country k.

and c_i^k is given as:

$$c_i^k = \frac{\left(\sum_j \sum_k e_i^{kj} D_i^j \right) f}{P_i - \sum_{g=G_i^k+1}^{H_i} a_{gi} P_g - v_{Ji} K r^k - v_{2i} s_2^k - Y_{id}^k - L_i^k - F_i^k} \tag{28}$$

where:

e_i^{kj} = cost of transportation of good i from country k to country j.

D_i^j = the amount of good i demanded by country j as a fraction of the total amount of good i demanded.

f = reciprocal of economy wide shadow exchange rate.

denominator equals the international value added in process i in country k. See page 46 for detailed notation.

In the formulation of the objective function it is implicitly assumed that production costs more than outweigh transport costs so that only one country can be the recipient of one industry. Therefore for each country only the domestic value and the sum of transport costs, per unit of international value added, of satisfying the whole area is computed rather than the domestic value added and transport cost of satisfying each country independently. Although this is consistent with the objective of allocating industries as integers, corrections should be made by dividing and redefining industries if transport costs become significant enough to warrant the sacrifice of economies of scale in favor of several production locations.

VI

The minimizing function, equation 15, is constrained by a monopoly and various distributional constraints. Capacity constraints are not included because of the assumption that the member countries have enough unemployed resources available to undertake the assigned projects. Indeed, the member countries would not be very concerned with the distribution of industries if capacity limitations prevented them from engaging in any of the industries to be allocated. Market requirement constraints are not necessary since the quantities to be demanded can be projected and the plants to be installed can be built accordingly. The monopoly constraint is introduced so that one given industry is assigned to only one country. This constraint takes the form of a dichotomous variable that takes on the value of one, when the industry is assigned to the country, and takes on the value of zero otherwise.

$$Z_i^k = (1, 0) \qquad (29)$$

VII

The participating countries of a free trade area in which sectorial programs of industrial development are implemented may have divergent views with respect to the benefits to be derived from these programs. Thus, it could be conceived that the various countries would view their benefits as consisting of industrialization, increases in income, increases in investment, improvements in the balance of payments, technological advancement, and the generation of employment. Furthermore it is also possible to envision any number of distributional constraints because positive economics does not provide guidelines to formulate these constraints in order to obtain an optimal distribution of benefits. The only generally accepted position on the problem of benefit distribution is the normative stipulation that the poorer members should receive somewhat more than their proportional share of benefits. Several distributional constraints that would appear acceptable to all members are formulated here.

The simplest allocation of industries in a free trade area would be achieved by assigning to each country an equal number of industries. This would probably be a very acceptable distribution if all countries had equal populations and equal incomes and all industries were equally important. If however, population sizes and incomes were not equal for all countries, then the poorer countries with lower than average per capita incomes would prefer an allocation scheme based on population, while the richer countries with greater than average per capita incomes would favor a scheme based on country incomes. Therefore, without introducing normative distributional weights, the upper and lower bounds of acceptable distributions for the richer and poorer countries can be formulated. The least the poorer countries would be willing to accept would be a repartition according to the countries' incomes. This lower bound imposed by the poorer countries is also the upper bound for the richer ones. Thus, the most the rich countries could expect would be a system of distribution that determined the numbers of industries to be assigned on the basis of the countries' incomes. The lower bound on number of industries assigned acceptable to the richer countries and the upper bound for the poorer ones would be given by an allocation proportionate to population. Thus, if the poorer countries are $m = 1$, $\ldots, K^*$ and the richer are $m = K^*+1, \ldots, K$, then the constraints on the numbers of industries allocated to the countries can be written as lower bound for countries with smaller than average incomes per capita as shown in equation **30**:

$$\sum_i Z_i^k \geqslant \frac{Y^k}{Y^M} \sum_k \sum_i Z_i^k \tag{30}$$

for all $m = 1 \ldots K^*$

And lower bound for countries with larger than average incomes per capita as shown in equation **31**:

$$\sum_i Z_i^k \geqslant \frac{\text{pop } k}{\text{pop } M} \sum_k \sum_i Z_i^k \tag{31}$$

for all countries $m = K^* + 1 \ldots K$

Z_i^k = dichotomous variable taking on the value of one or zero depending on whether industry i is assigned to country k or not.

Y^k = income of country k.

Y^M = income of the free trade area.

pop k = population of country k.

pop M = population of the free trade area.

The number of industries assigned a country represents only a very rough index of the benefits gained from a particular distribution. More realistically the member countries would probably be more interested in the increases in incomes to be expected from the industries received. These gains in incomes can be proportional to the gains in value added due to the establishment of the integration industries and therefore it is sufficient to set guidelines for the distribution of these values added. As in the case of the number of industries' constraints, only upper and lower distributional bounds can be formulated. The lower bound acceptable to the relatively richer countries would be given by an assignment of gains in incomes proportional to populations. The lower bound acceptable to the relatively poorer countries would be set by an allocation according to income. These constraints would be expressed as lower bound for countries with smaller than average incomes per capita:[12]

$$
\sum_i \left[P_i (1 + t_i^k) - \sum_{g = G_i^k + 1}^{H_i} a_{gi} P_g (1 + t_g^k) - \left(v_{Ji} + \sum_{g=1}^{G_i^k} a_{gi} v_{Jg} \right) Kr^k \right.
$$

$$
\left. - \left(v_{2i} + \sum_{g=1}^{G_i^k} a_{gi} v_{2g} \right) s_2^k \right] Z_i^k D_i \geq \frac{Y^k}{Y^M} \sum_k \sum_i \left[P_i (1 + t_i^k) \right.
$$

$$
- \sum_{g = G_i^k + 1}^{H_i} a_{gi} P_g (1 + t_g^k) - \left(v_{Ji} + \sum_{g=1}^{G_i^k} a_{gi} v_{Jg} \right) Kr^k - \left(v_{2i} + \right.
$$

$$
\left. \left. \sum_{g=1}^{G_i^k} a_{gi} v_{2g} \right) s_2^k \right] Z_i^k D_i \tag{32}
$$

for all $m = 1 \ldots K^*$

These constraints would be expressed as lower bound for countries with larger than average incomes per capita:

$$\sum_i \left[P_i (1 + t_i^k) - \sum_{g=G_i^k+1}^{H_i} a_{gi} P_g (1 + t_g^k) - \left(v_{Ji} + \sum_{g=1}^{G_i^k} a_{gi} v_{Jg} \right) Kr^k \right.$$

$$\left. - \left(v_{2i} + \sum_{g=1}^{G_i^k} a_{gi} v_{2g} \right) s_2^k \right] Z_i^k D_i \geq \frac{\text{pop } k}{\text{pop } M} \sum_k \sum_i \left[P_i (1 + t_i^k) \right.$$

$$- \sum_{g=G_i^k+1}^{H_i} a_{gi} P_g (1 + t_g^k) - \left(v_{Ji} + \sum_{g=1}^{G_i^k} a_{gi} v_{Jg} \right) Kr^k$$

$$\left. - \left(v_{2i} + \sum_{g=1}^{G_i^k} a_{gi} v_{2g} \right) s_2^k \right] Z_i^k D_i \tag{33}$$

for all countries $m = K^* + 1, \ldots, K$

P_i = international price of good i.

t_i^k = tariff on good i in country k.

a_{gi} = amount of input g necessary for the production of one unit of good i in physical units.

P_g = international price of input good g.

t_g^k = tariff on input good g in country k.

v_{Ji} = amount of imported capital necessary for the production of one unit of i.

v_{Jg} = amount of imported capital necessary for the production of input good g.

K = international price of capital.

r^k = rate of return to capital.

v_{2i} = amount of factor 2, foreign factors, employed in the production of one unit of good i.

v_{2g} = the amount of foreign factors necessary for the production of input good g.

s_2^k = repatriated returns to foreign factors of production.

Z_i^k = dichotomous variable assuming the value of one when the industry i is assigned to country k and zero otherwise.

D_i = total free trade area demand for product i.

Y^k = income of country k.

Y^M = income of the free trade area.

pop k = population of country k.

pop M = population of the free trade area.

$g = 1, \ldots, G_i^k$ = domestic goods utilized in the production of good i in country k.

$g = G_i^k + 1, \ldots, H_i$ = imported goods utilized in the production of good i in country k.

With respect to investment, the member countries might have either of two objectives in mind: the distribution of total, direct and indirect, investment caused by the integration industries *or* the distribution of the direct investment in the integration industries. The distribution of the total investment would lead to a constraint similar to the value added distribution constraint if the capital output ratios are similar in the various countries. The other objective of distributing the direct investment is probably more important to the member countries and will also constitute an additional rather than a superfluous constraint. However, as in the case of the value added constraint, only upper and lower bounds are formulated.

Lower bound for the countries with relatively *low* incomes per capita:

$$\sum_i I_i\, Z_i^k \geqslant \frac{Y^k}{Y^M} \sum_k \sum_i I_i Z_i^k \tag{34}$$

for countries $m = 1 \ldots K^*$

Lower bound for the countries with relatively *high* incomes per capita:

$$\sum_i I_i\, Z_i^k \geqslant \frac{\text{pop } k}{\text{pop } M} \sum_k \sum_i I_i Z_i^k \tag{35}$$

for countries $m = K^* + 1 \ldots K$

I_i = investment necessary to produce i for the free trade area.

Z_i^k = dichotomous variable.

Y^k = income of country k.

Y^M = income of the free trade area.

pop k = population of country k.

pop M = population of the free trade area.

Another important benefit from integration is the relaxation of the pressure on the balance of payments of the area due to import substitution. Here, the question of whether import substitution does actually ease the pressure on the balance of payments is not considered and it is simply assumed that it does. The foreign exchange saved through import substitution can be divided in many ways. However, it seems plausible that no one country would wish to lose foreign exchange to any of the other countries and therefore another distributional criterion could be sales equalization: the sales of any one country to the area are equal to the country's purchases from the area.

The sales equalization constraint may also be defended on the basis that the purchases of member countries' products at higher than world prices, because of protective tariffs, involve real subsidies to the selling countries. In an integration scheme where the economies are of different sizes and incomes, it would be expected that there would be a net transfer of resources from the smaller and/or poorer countries to the larger and/or richer countries if trade flows are not equated. Further, this criterion would not necessarily be incompatible with different rates of trade expansion and the different sized countries need not limit their expansion to the rate of the small countries but may trade among each other. This criterion can be imposed in practice since it is easily measurable. This constraint may be expressed as:

$$\sum_{j \neq k} \sum_i D_i^j Z_i^k - \sum_{j \neq k} \sum_i D_i^k Z_i^j = |F| \tag{36}$$

for all countries k

D_i^j = demand for product i by country j.

Z_i^k = dichotomous variable.

E = constant reflecting an allowable margin of error.

In spite of the advantages of the trade equalization criterion it is possible to suggest a superior criterion, subsidy equalization, which directly rather than indirectly imposes limits on the net transfer of resources from one country to another in the form of subsidies. This criterion would equate the country's subsidization of the area with the area's subsidization of the country. The advantages of this are that it prevents the smaller countries from subsidizing the larger ones and it provides an incentive to become a low-cost producer. This criterion is superior to the sales equalization constraint if the free trade area does not adopt a uniform common external tariff. It can be formulated as:

$$\sum_{j \neq k} \sum_i u_i^k D_i^j Z_i^k - \sum_{j \neq k} \sum_i u_i^j D_i^k Z_i^j = |F| \tag{37}$$

where

$$u_i^k = \frac{P_i^k - P_i^w}{P_i^w}$$

P_i^k = price of good i in country k.

P_i^w = world price of good i.

D_i^j = demand for product i by country j.

Z_i^k = dichotomous variable.

F = constant reflecting an allowable margin of error.

A technological distribution constraint also seems necessary since often no country desires to lag behind or be dependent on another for any type of technology. Further, the member countries may believe that should the market break up, it would be easier to transform the industry within the sector to produce the other products of the sector than it would be to transform the industries of a sector to produce the goods of other sectors. Therefore, it may be appropriate to assign each country at least one industry in each sector even though this may considerably impair the efficiency of the extended market. Dividing the industries of a sector into q subsectors such that $i^* = 1 \ldots q$, the technology distribution constraint can be formulated as:

$$\sum_{i \in i^*} Z_i^k \geqslant 0 \tag{38}$$

for all k and for all subsectors $i^* = 1 \ldots q$.

A generation of employment constraint will not be formulated because the industries allocated might differ in the amounts and types of employment offered. Although this could be formulated the implementation of the constraint might prove impractical. However, the industries allocated presumably have similar manpower needs and the amounts of employment generated would be proportional to either the total values added or to the direct investments in the integration industries and therefore an employment generation constraint would probably be redundant.

VIII

The model as presented, however, will only provide an approximate indication as to how to allocate integration industries in a free trade area and the results should not be taken as definitive. Rather, corrections should be made for a number of elements not considered in the model and for possible biases introduced by the method suggested for determining comparative costs and allocating industries. Nevertheless, allowing for these limitations, in practice the model remains a very useful tool for examining and proposing particular integration industry allocations.

The industry assignments proposed by the implementation of the model described should be modified for dynamic considerations. The model is a static model that does not incorporate any dynamic changes brought about by the suggested allocation. This criticism, however, would not be particular to this model since dynamic considerations would be difficult to incorporate in any but the most general and all-encompassing models for a free trade area.

A more important criticism of the model is that it does not allow for intraregional trade in inputs. This restriction does require that the results be modified to correct for errors introduced because of this limitation. However, it is expected that, in general, the effort necessary for individual corrections for a few such traded inputs would not warrant the extension of the model with all the accompanying complications.

Another criticism of the model is that in practice if allocations are made using DRCs, computed as ERP+1, based on current tariffs in the various member countries, the further assumption of no economies of scale creeps in. Theoretically the model allows for economies of scale that would manifest themselves through changing input coefficients and changing prices, and consequently changing optimal tariffs.[13] In practice, however, it is expected that each country would have set its tariffs with a certain protection for a certain scale of operations in mind. Then in comparing DRCs for different countries we would be implicitly assuming away economies of scale. This shortcoming is not very grave if similar linear economies of scale are present in all the industries considered because the comparative cost ranking will not be affected.

In the model industries are allocated on the basis of comparative costs as determined from a comparison of DRCs for the various industries in the various countries. These DRCs are calculated from goods prices taken to be equal to international prices plus tariffs. Theory indicates that domestic market prices should be equal to the international prices plus the respective tariffs, and the empirical work by Norman[14] suggests that this is indeed the case. However, if domestic prices are not equal to international prices plus tariffs, corrections should be made if the divergence between the two sets is not similar across all goods in all countries. If the divergence between domestic prices and international prices plus tariffs is proportionately constant for all goods in all countries then, as in the case of economies of scale, the comparative cost ranking is not affected.

4 THE PETROCHEMICAL INDUSTRY AND THE ANDEAN COMMON MARKET

In the last chapter a model was developed to allocate the industries of the sectorial programs of industrial development among the member countries of a free trade area so as to minimize the cost of supplying the area with the products of these industries. This cost minimization objective is constrained by distributional requirements. This model is implemented both to analyze the industry allocation of the petrochemical program of the Andean Common Market and to test the validity of the model in policy situations.

The model can be applied to the Andean Common Market because, even though its name implies that it is a common market, the group can best be classified as a free trade area.[1] Beyond an initial agreement on a minimum common external tariff, it was impossible to implement a common external tariff, negotiations were stalled, and the deadline for the negotiation and establishment of common external tariffs was postponed.[2] Furthermore, even though common external tariffs have been formulated for the petrochemical sector, these will not be completely in effect—even though they will be approached in a linear manner—until 1980 in Colombia, Chile, Peru, and Venezuela and until 1985 in Bolivia and Ecuador.[3]

In this chapter the general characteristics of the petrochemical industry will be discussed. Next, the reasons for the selection of the petrochemical program from the two approved Sectorial Programs of Industrial Development of the Andean Common Market will be listed. Lastly, the importance of the petrochemical sector in the Andean Common Market will be discussed and the industry allocation scheme ratified by the Comision del Acuerdo de Cartagena by means of their Decision 91[4] will be described.

I

Before examining the reasons for selecting the petrochemical industry for the implementation of the model and analyzing the petrochemical industry in the Andean Common Market and the industry allocations specifically it is helpful to consider briefly the salient characteristics of the petrochemical industry. It is necessary to keep in mind these characteristics because these help to determine the usefulness of data and the rationality of both the industry allocation scheme developed by the Junta del Acuerdo de Cartagena and of the alternative allocations obtained with the model.

The petrochemical industry is a relatively new industry that derives its name from the utilization of petroleum and natural gas as the basic inputs for the production of certain organic chemicals. Thus, until fifty years ago the only sources of organic chemicals were the following:

Coal carbonization for coal tar distillation and the production of benzene, toluene, xylenes, and naphthalenes.
Wood distillation to obtain acetic acid, formaldehyde, acetone, and others.
Alcoholic fermentation: the formation of alcohol from sugar by yeasts.
Reaction of calcium carbide with water to produce acetylene, a starting material for a number of organic syntheses.[5]

The production in industrial quantities of organic chemicals based on petroleum began in 1920 with the production of isopropyl alcohol. The petrochemical industry originated in the United States because of the availability of raw material resources such as petroleum and natural gas and because of the existence of a substantial market for the chemical products. However, the rapid development of the petrochemical industry in the United States can be mostly attributed to the availability of a large number of refinery by-products obtained from the distillation of oil to produce naphtha, or straight-run gasoline; the catalytic reforming of naphtha to produce higher octane gasolines; and the catalytic cracking of the heavier oil fractions to increase the gasoline recovery ratio so as to meet the rapidly expanding demand for motor fuel. The Second World War and the consequent scarcity of natural rubber provided added impetus to the industry by creating the need for synthetic rubber. The effort applied in developing synthetic rubber had important spillover effects in terms of developments in the areas of plastics, solvents, and textile fibers. The United States' advantage in the petrochemical industry has been maintained in spite of the rapid growth of the industry in Europe during the past thirty years and the United States remains the largest producer of petrochemicals.

A distinguishing characteristic of the petrochemical industry is the wide range of application of its products.[6] Thus from its meager beginning the petrochemical industry has expanded into a pervasive industry indispensable in modern times: the names of the companies producing petrochemicals—DuPont, Celanese, Union Carbide, etc.—have become household words and the products are utilized in the production and distribution of nearly all products in the market today. Thus petrochemicals are employed in the packaging of food, in the production of nearly all household goods, from containers to refrigerators to radios and televisions, in the apparel industry in the form of synthetic fibers, in the construction industry in the form of water pipes and wire insulation, and in the automotive industry as parts in distributors and instrument panels, as well as tires.

Although smaller than the petroleum industry, the petrochemical industry is also characterized by its large scale of operations. Production quantities are given in millions of pounds or in thousands of tons. Plants are large because of economies of scale: capital investment related charges per ton of product decrease with plant size; larger volumes make it possible to take advantage of modern advances in automatic control, materials handling, and equipment design.

The products of the petrochemical industry are mainly homogeneous. Thus products are often industrially marketed in accordance with only one set of specifications with respect to form, purity, and presence of contaminating compounds.

The petrochemical industry is highly capital intensive and the initial investment in plant and equipment is high. The industry is not a large employer of labor. In many instances the production processes are continuous and automatically controlled and the need for manual work is limited. There is, however, a need for skilled labor because the industry can be characterized as being very technical and its dependence on scientific knowledge is only superseded by the electronics and aerospace industries. Nevertheless, the capital related charges per unit of production are often five and six times greater than the labor costs.

The petrochemical industry also demonstrates a high rate of innovation: new products and new processes mark the development of the industry from year to year. New products are invented and commercialized on a yearly basis. The processes by which products are manufactured also are frequently improved: the main process for manufacturing phenol, for example, has been radically changed three times during the past thirty years.

Another feature of the petrochemical industry is that it is a major user of energy. Energy costs figure high in the value of petrochemicals because the transformation of the inputs into the desired products by means of chemical reactions most often consumes great amounts of heat. The costs of energy are only slightly smaller than the charges for capital.

Lastly, it is noted that the petrochemical industry is concentrated in the developed countries. The concentration is the result of the fact that the industry was developed in these countries because in these countries there was a large effective demand for petrochemicals. In the United States the industry was based on the availability of cheap refinery by-products that resulted from the production of gasoline. The requirement of a large demand for motor fuel was eliminated by the development of cracking units specially designed to produce the olefinic gas streams that are the inputs to the petrochemical industry. The European petrochemical industry is based on inputs derived from such cracking units.

The petrochemical industry poses a great attraction to many less developed countries. Less developed countries have traditionally imported petrochemicals and the growth in the demand has aggravated the balance of payments problems. Furthermore, since many LDCs have oil that can be transformed in cracking units into the olefins necessary for the petrochemical industry, the LDCs expect the costs of domestic production to be competitive with those in the industrialized countries. The desire to save foreign exchange, the availability of raw materials and the desire for industrialization make petrochemical industries good candidates for import substituting industrialization.

II

The petrochemical program was selected for the implementation of the model because the characteristics of the petrochemical industry make this program the easiest to analyze. The petrochemical program of sectorial development is one of two programs that have been formulated by the Junta del Acuerdo de Cartagena and have been ratified by the member countries.[7] The other program that has been approved is the metal working program. The products of the petrochemical industry, unlike those of the metal working industry, are generally standardized and homogeneous and make the petrochemical program more amenable to analysis.

The homogeneity of the products of the petrochemical industry makes it possible to establish meaningful prices for petrochemical products. There is no product differentiation in the petrochemical industry and given a fair degree of competition, it is expected that prices reflect the level of costs.

Furthermore, because the products are homogeneous it is found that often there is only one main process for producing each of the products. Therefore the production coefficients can be easily determined. The determination of these coefficients is simplified by the fact that these production processes are patented and the coefficients published. Also the chemistry of the products is general knowledge and the approximate amounts of inputs could be determined by balancing the chemical reaction equations.

Another reason for selecting the petrochemical sector rather than the metal working sector is that the former is better suited for cooperation schemes than the latter. This is because the industries of the petrochemical sector are generally characterized by large minimum efficient scales of production. That is, the industries of the petrochemical sector exhibit significant economies of scale until a certain size plant is reached.[8,9]

III

The Sectorial Programs of Industrial Development of the Andean Common Market are designed to take advantage of the expanded market to further import substituting industrialization. The petrochemical industry was selected for such an import substituting program because of the area's endowment with the necessary raw materials and because of the pressure of petrochemical imports on the balance of payments. Although only Venezuela, Peru, and Ecuador have large exportable surpluses of oil, all the member countries produce oil. Chile's limited oil production is compensated by its production of natural gas. Bolivia also has natural gas and is South America's first major gas exporting country. It is hoped that the development of a petrochemical industry will also help to save foreign exchange: in 1970 petrochemical imports accounted for 17 percent of the area's imports of manufactures.[10] The importance of the petrochemical program of industrial development is difficult to ascertain. The Junta del Acuerdo de Cartagena (JUNAC), the technical body of the Agreement, estimates that the demand for products from the petrochemical industries was $480 million in 1975 and projected that it would grow at an average of 11.4 percent per year. The 1975 demand was met by $200 million worth of domestic production and $280 million worth of imports. JUNAC projected the 1985 demand to be met totally by domestic production. The figures, however, refer to the whole petrochemical program, which includes a number of industries that were not allocated and whose inclusion is rather meaningless as explained in the next section.

The investment requirements as estimated by JUNAC amounted to $2500 million.[11] This total was divided into the purchases of technology, the purchases of equipment, and other expenditures. The amount to be spent on technology purchases, which includes licensing and process engineering, as well as technical services, was estimated to be $500 million to correspond to $300 million of imports and $200 million of domestic purchases. The equipment expenditure was expected to be $800 million, composed of $400 million worth of imports and $400 million of locally supplied inputs. In the category of other expenditures were included buildings, assemblies, and installations. The imported content of this expenditure was expected to be $300 million while the domestic contribution was $900 million. Again, however, these figures refer to investments in the whole petrochemical sector rather than to investments in the allocated industries.

The estimates and projections of JUNAC are questionable and are contradicted by preliminary country estimates with respect to the expected value of sales in 1985 and with respect to the required investments. The expected value of sales in 1985 in dollars of 1975 as projected by JUNAC was distributed as follows:[12]

Bolivia	$ 120 million/year	8%
Chile	$ 230 million/year	15%
Colombia	$ 370 million/year	25%
Ecuador	$ 160 million/year	11%
Peru	$ 260 million/year	17%
Venezuela	$ 360 million/year	24%
	$1500 million/year	100%

The estimated required investment in dollars of 1975 was distributed as follows:[13]

Bolivia	$ 250 million	10%
Chile	$ 380 million	15%
Colombia	$ 600 million	24%
Ecuador	$ 320 million	13%
Peru	$ 420 million	17%
Venezuela	$ 530 million	21%
	$2500 million	100%

These estimates are contradicted by preliminary country estimates of Bolivia, Chile, Ecuador, and Venezuela; similar estimates were not available for Colombia and Peru. Thus the Bolivian Ministry of Energy estimated that the necessary investment in the petrochemical sector in Bolivia would be $640 million; the estimate of sales in 1985 was $340 million.[14] The Association for Chemical Industrialists of Chile estimated that the necessary investment in Chile would be $290 million and that the industry would gross $680 million/year in 1985.[15] The Ecuadorian Ministry of Industry, Commerce and Integration estimated the required investment to be $400 million and sales in 1985 to be $600 million.[16] The Institute of Foreign Commerce of Venezuela estimated that the required investment would be $530 million and that the demand for Venezuela's products in 1985 would be $360 million.[17] However, the reliability of these preliminary estimates is also questionable and probably reflects overoptimistic expectations.

The aforementioned demand and investment estimates of the Junta del Acuerdo de Cartagena and the individual member countries thus reveal in a very rough way the order of magnitude of the petrochemical program. However, these estimates are for the whole sector and include the investment requirements and sales estimates of a number of industries that were not allocated.

IV

The estimates of the importance of the petrochemical program by JUNAC and the member countries are inflated by the inclusion in the program of a number of industries that are not expected to be established or whose products are not expected to be traded in the expanded market. The industries of the petrochemical program were divided into two groups and only the industries of one group were allocated. The industries of the second group were not allocated and were designated as free to locate anywhere in the area.[18]

The concern in this text is with the allocated industries. The non-allocated industries can basically be divided into two groups: those for which there is no demand and the ones that are basic to the petrochemical industry. The very specialized industries for whose products there is only a limited demand will probably not be established and therefore their production as well as investment requirements need not be considered. The basic industries need also not be considered since it is expected that the member countries will all develop these industries in an autarkic fashion. Therefore only the products of the allocated industries will enter the expanded market. The inclusion of non-allocated industries in the program is therefore meaningless.

V

The demand for products of the allocated industries, that is those industries that form the core of the petrochemical program and that are the subject of analysis of this text, was established by the author to be $245 million in 1974.[19] This estimate is based on the area's demand for imports and on the imputed amount of domestic production. The demand for imports of the products of the assigned industries was estimated by the author to be $88 million. The value of the domestic production at international prices of these same products was estimated to be $157 million.

The sum of the member countries' demands for the products allocated in the petrochemical program was calculated from United States export data. In the next chapter the utilization of U.S. export data to determine the area's imports is justified.

The domestic production of the products of the allocated industries in 1974 was estimated by the author to be $157 million. This optimistic estimate was based on the installed capacity of industries that were allocated. It was assumed that the average capacity utilization of the smaller and older plants and the larger and newer plants just brought on stream is 80 percent. This optimistic assumption was employed because it was impossible to determine varying degrees of capacity utilization in different industries in different countries. The assumption has the advantage that particular demands for individual products will not be underestimated and that probable overestimates serve to emphasize the size and possibilities of the expanded market. The subjects of demand estimation and capacity utilization will be discussed in more detail in the next chapter.

The value of the 1985 demand valued at 1975 international prices for the products of the allocated industries was projected by the author to be $860 million. This projection was based on a demand growth rate of 11.4 percent per year, the optimistic growth rate expected by the Junta del Acuerdo de Cartagena.

The investment requirement for additional plants to satisfy the demands of the allocated industries was estimated to be $676 million. This estimate is based on the assumption of an 80 percent capacity utilization and on the allocation of industries designed by the Junta. That is, the investment requirement is of the order of $676 million because the industries were not assigned undivided to the member countries but rather assigned to an average of four countries. If the industries had been assigned wholly, economies of scale would have lowered the investment requirements to $468 million. The determination of investment requirements is discussed in detail in the next chapter.

VI

The Junta del Acuerdo de Cartagena designed a petrochemical program in which 56 industries were allocated among the six member countries. Table 4.01 summarizes these allocations.[20]

The industry allocation designed by the Junta can however be very much simplified by:

Aggregating products from the same industry into one industry.

Table 4.01. Industry Allocation by the Junta del Acuerdo de Cartagena

Industry	Bolivia	Chile	Colombia	Ecuador	Peru	Venezuela
Carbon Black			X		X	X
Sodium Cyanide		X			X	X
Potassium Cyanide		X			X	X
Calcium Cyanide		X			X	X
Styrene	X					X
Fluorocarbons		X				X
Ethylene Dichloride	X	X	X	X	X	X
Vinyl Chloride	X	X	X	X	X	X
Trichloroethylene		X				X
Perchloroethylene		X				X
Methanol						X
Isopropyl Alcohol		X			X	
Butyl Alcohol		X				
Isobutyl Alcohol		X				
2-Ethyl-Hexyl Alcohol		X				
Ethylene Glycol				X		
Propylene Glycol	X					X
Pentaerythritol		X				
Phenol	X					
Diethylene Glycol				X		
Dipropylene Glycol	X					X
Triethylene Glycol				X		
Propylene Glycol Ethers	X					X
Ethylene Glycol Ethers				X		
Ethylene Oxide				X		
Propylene Oxide	X					X
Vinyl Acetate Monomer		X				

	Col 1	Col 2	Col 3	Col 4	Col 5
Methyl Methacrylate				X	
Other Methacrylic Acid				X	
Maleic Anhydride			X		
Terephthalic Acid			X		
Phthalic Anhydride	X		X	X	X
Dimethyl Terephthalate			X		
Monoethanolamine			X		
Diethanolamine			X		
Triethanolamine			X		
Acrylonitrile		X			X
2,4 Tolylene Diisocyanate	X				
Caprolactam			X	X	
Monoethers of Ethylene Glycol of 11 carbons or more	X		X		
Polyethylene Glycols			X		X
Polypropylene Glycols					X
Polyethylene Low Density	X	X	X	X	X
Polyethylene High Density	X		X	X	
Polystyrene	X	X	X	X	X
ABS, SAN resins	X		X	X	
Polyvinyl Chloride Emulsion	X		X	X	X
Polyvinyl Chloride Suspension	X	X	X	X	X
Polyvinyl Chloroacetate	X	X	X	X	X
Polyacrylonitrile		X	X	X	
Polypropylene			X		X
Styrene-Butadiene Rubber	X		X	X	
Styrene-Butadiene Rubber Latex					
Acrylic Fibers	X		X	X	
Cables for Acrylic Fibers		X	X	X	

Integrating those industries where vertical integration is the rule.

Eliminating those industries for whose products there is very little or no demand.[21]

The number of industries allocated can be reduced by integrating as one industry those industries that are technically one industry. A set of industries is technically one industry if the products of these industries are generally produced in the same plant and the products are produced simultaneously in the same process. Thus it is meaningless to separate ethanolamines into monoethanolamine, diethanolamine, and triethanolamine. Similarly, trichloroethylene and perchloroethylene should also be treated as one industry. Ethylene glycol, diethylene glycol, triethylene glycol, and polyethylene glycol are all simultaneously produced by the hydration of ethylene oxide. The hydration of propylene oxide yields propylene glycol, dipropylene glycol, and polypropylene glycol. Butyl and isobutyl alcohols are simultaneously produced and should therefore be considered together.[22]

In addition to the industries that are technically one industry, the high and low density polyethylene industries were integrated because they use the same inputs and because it was assumed that if one country had a comparative advantage in one it would also demonstrate a comparative advantage in the other. The same reason served as the rationale for integrating the emulsion and suspension polyvinyl chloride industries and the SBR and SBR latex industries. Dimethyl terephthalate and terephthalic acid were also grouped as one industry. The reason for this grouping is that the products are produced with similar inputs and have very similar properties and uses. Finally, the acrylic fibers industry generally also produces cables for acrylic fibers and thus the two industries were integrated.

Among the industries allocated are a number of industries that can be defined separately but that are generally integrated. Therefore it makes no sense to allocate these industries separately. Thus, in general, producers of vinyl chloride monomer have a captive source of ethylene dichloride and of the total of ethylene dichloride produced, 77 percent is utilized to produce vinyl chloride monomer.[23] Furthermore, 97 percent of the vinyl chloride monomer produced is used to produce polyvinyl chloride.[24] Therefore, the ethylene dichloride, vinyl chloride, and polyvinyl chloride industries should be treated as one industry. Similarly, most of the polystyrene capacity is owned by the monomer producers[25] and 56 percent of the production of styrene is used to make polystyrene and the integration of these two industries can be justified. Fifty-nine percent of the production of acrylonitrile is used to produce acrylic fibers. Polyacrylonitrile should also be incorporated into acrylic fibers because many of the acrylic fibers are made from this polymer of acrylonitrile. In the same way, ethylene oxide and ethylene glycols, as well as propylene oxide and propylene glycol, should be vertically integrated and treated as single industries.

The elimination of the industries whose products are not demanded further simplifies the industry allocation task. Thus the demands for potassium and calcium cyanide are very small. Other industries that could be eliminated because of limited demand are: 2-ethyl-hexyl alcohol, pentaerythritol, propylene and ethylene glycol ethers, vinyl acetate monomer, methacrylic acid esters different from methyl methacrylate, maleic anhydride, monoethers of ethylene glycol obtained from alcohols with eleven or more carbons, and polyvinyl chloracetate.

Introducing the above listed simplifications the industry allocation desired by JUNAC is summarized in Table 4.02.[26]

The allocation of industries designed by JUNAC does not reveal any given pattern. Eight of the twenty-two industries were allocated to only one country: Chile, Ecuador, and Venezuela were exclusively assigned two industries each and Bolivia and Colombia were favored with one each. Peru was not assigned any industry exclusively, but it must be noted that only Peru can have an integrated acrylic fibers industry since acrylonitrile was assigned to it; the value to Colombia of the acrylic fibers industry is questionable. In this scheme there is also the rather indefinite allocation of polystyrene to all countries while only Bolivia and Venezuela were allocated styrene. The other industries that should be vertically integrated were assigned more consistently: thus all countries were assigned ethylene dichloride, vinyl chloride monomer, and polyvinyl chloride; Bolivia and Venezuela were both assigned propylene oxide and propylene glycols; and Ecuador was assigned ethylene oxide and ethylene glycols.

The remaining industries were all assigned to two or more countries. The allocation of industries to more than one country limits the benefits that were to be derived from the establishment of larger units of production made possible by the extended market. The countries sharing industries are all expected to set up their own industries, which they are allowed to protect from competing industries in countries favored with the same allocation.

The allocation of industries designed by the Junta del Acuerdo de Cartagena will be further analyzed when it is compared to industry allocations devised with the aid of the model presented in the last chapter. The model is implemented to determine industry allocations in the two chapters following the next chapter. The next chapter is devoted to a discussion of the products, and of the data utilized for the computation of domestic resource costs.

Table 4.02. Simplified Industry Allocation by the Junta del Acuerdo de Cartagena

Industry	Bolivia	Chile	Colombia	Ecuador	Peru	Venezuela
Carbon black			X		X	X
Sodium cyanide		X			X	
Tri, perchloroethylene		X				X
Isopropyl Alcohol		X			X	X
Butanol		X				
Ethylene Glycols				X		
Propylene Glycols	X					X
Phenol	X					
Methyl Methacrylate		X				
Phthalic Anhydride	X	X	X	X	X	X
Dimethyl Terephthalate			X			
Ethanolamines				X		
2,4 Tolylene Diisocyanate						X
Caprolactam			X	X		
Polyethylene	X	X	X	X	X	X
Polystyrene	X	X	X	X	X	X
ABS, SAN resins			X	X		
Polyvinyl Chloride	X	X	X	X	X	X
Polypropylene	X	X		X		
SBR, SBR Latex			X		X	X
Acrylic Fibers			X		X	
Methanol						X

5 THE DATA FRAMEWORK REQUIRED FOR THE IMPLEMENTATION OF THE MODEL

The last chapter provided a general description of the petrochemical industry and an analysis of the petrochemical program industry allocation scheme of the Junta del Acuerdo de Cartagena. This industrial allocation scheme was simplified by eliminating some industries and aggregating and integrating others into more meaningful entities.

The purpose of this chapter is to present the estimates of the domestic resource cost (DRC) of foreign exchange in each of the industrial entities of the simplified allocation program in each of the countries. These estimates of DRCs are introduced into the model in the next two chapters to determine alternative allocations of industries and to test the usefulness of the model in simplifying the task of allocating the industries of the Sectorial Programs of Industrial Development among the member countries.

In Appendix A the industries will be described. The technological aspects of production are considered and the input coefficients are determined. The most important uses of the products are also presented.

The international prices of the products of the industries to be allocated are established in the first section. First, the nature and sources of the prices are discussed. Second, the specifications of the products and the services offered for the listed per unit prices of the products are considered.

Next, the tariffs in the different countries for the different products and their inputs are presented. The limitations inherent in the utilization of tariffs as measures of protection when there are other unquantifiable restrictions on imports are then discussed. It is also attempted to determine the effect that the usage of only tariffs will have on the model.

The third section is devoted to a description of the estimation of the demands for the various products in the various countries. These demands were estimated from United States' exports of the products to the member countries and from the installed capacities to produce these products in the member countries. Demand projections were then made to establish the demands in 1985.

The estimates of the demands in 1985 were then used to determine the investment requirements necessary for the satisfaction of the various products' demands in 1985. The fourth section is devoted to a discussion of the data and methods employed to determine these demands.

Given the investment requirements it is next necessary to determine the amounts that are to be subtracted from both the measures of domestic value added and of the measure of international value added for rent to imported capital and the return to foreign owned capital in the calculation of the domestic resource cost for each product in each country. Section V is devoted to the estimation of the payments to capital that cannot be considered part of the domestic value added. The expected effects on the estimates of DRCs of the inclusion of these factors are analyzed.

Given the data delineated above and assuming for the time being that the transport costs of the finished goods are zero, the DRC for each product in each country can be estimated. This DRC, with zero transportation costs, is utilized in the next chapters to determine a set of industry allocations that can be compared to industry allocations based on DRCs that include transportation costs. Thus the importance of transport costs to the industry allocations can be determined.

Transport costs are discussed in section VII. The available transport cost data are analyzed and representative costs are chosen for all routes between all pairs of member countries. Furthermore, because of the similarity of many of the products and the lack of consistent data, it was taken that all products on the same route would pay the same transport costs per ton.

In section VIII a new set of DRCs that include transport costs is estimated. The influence of the transport costs on the DRCs is analyzed. Also, the expected effect on the industry allocations of the next chapter is delineated.

In the tenth section general characteristics of the data and their effect on the model are considered. The limitations imposed on the model by the available data are described.

The products of the petrochemical industries are mostly homogeneous. However, the establishment of international prices involves the acceptance of a certain degree of error as the quoted prices of these products are not always the same. The differences in prices are often the result of differences in quantity, quality, and location. Price changes over time further complicate the determination of common international prices.

Petrochemical prices are reported on a regular basis in two journals: the *European Chemical News* and the *Chemical Marketing Reporter*. The first of these publications is mostly concerned with prices in Europe while the second reports on prices in the U.S. It was taken that the prices reported in the *Chemical Marketing Reporter* were the relevant prices for the calculation of the international value added in the production of the various products because the U.S. is the main producer of petrochemicals in the world and the mostly likely supplier of Latin American markets.

The prices reported in the *Chemical Marketing Reporter* do not represent bid or asked prices but rather negotiated prices. These negotiated prices often include services such as freight equalization or deliverance and therefore they are taken as the relevant c.i.f. prices for the Andean Common Market countries. The products and their respective prices are listed in Appendix B.

The prices of petroleum and petroleum products have exhibited rapid rates of increase in the past few years. Therefore for each of the products the price taken was given by the average of the prices at the beginning and end of 1975 in the hope of thereby reducing the error in the calculation of the international value added for each product. This error in the calculation of the international value added is minimized as errors due to price lags are partially eliminated.

II

In order to compute the domestic resource costs of production necessary for the implementation of the model developed in Chapter III it is necessary to compute the domestic value added in each of the industries in each of the countries. The domestic values added are determined on the basis of domestic prices as given by international prices plus tariffs.

The import tariffs of the countries were obtained from the tariff schedules published by these countries.[1] Although it is not necessary for the implementation of the model developed in Chapter III, the computation of the values added in each of the industries in each of the countries can be simplified if all tariffs are expressed in ad valorem terms. Thus, the specific duties imposed by Bolivia, Peru, and Venezuela in addition to ad valorem tariffs were converted to ad valorem terms and added to the respective ad valorem tariffs. The specific duties were converted to their ad valorem tariff equivalents by dividing the value of the duty for each product, expressed in domestic currency, by the exchange rate, and then by the c.i.f. price of the respective product. The exchange rate used for converting the duties imposed by Bolivia was that fixed by the Bolivian government for such duties.[2] The exchange rates used for Peru and Venezuela were those in effect in January of 1975.[3]

The protection granted by non-tariff restrictions was assumed to be the same in all countries. This assumption was made for two reasons: first the task of evaluating the values of non-tariff protection would be very difficult; and second, there is no a priori reason to believe that any one country would have a distinctly different set of non-tariff barriers. In Chapter VIII the implications of this assumption for the design of industry allocations are discussed.

The import tariffs for the relevant industries in the member countries are listed in Appendix C.

III

Data are also required concerning the demands of the various member countries for the products of the assigned petrochemical industries. These data are needed in order to estimate the investment requirements and the transportation costs for the later estimation of DRCs. The investment requirements for plants with sufficient capacity to meet the needs of the region are determined by the projected demands for the assigned products. The transportation costs are determined by the location of demands and production facilities.

The demands in 1974 by the member countries for the assigned products were determined from domestic production capacities and imports during that year. The domestic production capacities were given by the existence of plants in the member countries as reported in any of several sources.[4] The reported existence of plants was often contradictory as between sources as plans did not always materialize and therefore the data were modified to achieve consistency. Further, it was assumed that the plants in existence were operating at 80 percent capacity. An 80 percent capacity utilization figure is probably very optimistic given that the larger plants in the region were only very recently built but overestimates are probably preferable to underestimates.

The amounts of the products imported by the Andean Common Market countries could not be determined from import data for these countries because

Table 5.01. Demands for Products by Countries in 1985 (Tons)

Industry	Bolivia	Chile+	Colombia	Ecuador	Peru	Venezuela
Carbon black	—	523	64,676	—	419	39,036
Sodium cyanide	—	5,622	390	78	1,483	156
Tri- and Perchloethylene	—	521	3,881	290	405	637
Isopropanol	—	—	5,460	780	1,040	18,718
Butanol	—	13,986	2,220	—	1,776	4,218
Ethylene glycol	—	1,112	14,456	556	1,668	10,008
Propylene glycol	—	1,554	4,663	864	1,209	8,980
Phenol	—	—	5,868	—	—	2,934
Methyl methacrylate	—	904	3,279	452	1,017	5,654
Phthalic anhydride	—	2,487	5,166	—	765	10,714
Dimethyl terephthalate	—	38,294	32,338	—	—	14,467
Ethanolamines	—	—	1,127	129	258	1,706
2-4 Tolylene diisocyanide	—	316	759	822	506	3,920
Caprolactam*	—	—	45,952	—	—	—
Polyethylene	226	67,660	81,192	20,298	22,553	33,830
Polystyrene	60	7,568	9,687	3,633	5,146	4,238
ABS, SAN Resins	—	206	1,032	258	310	774
Polyvinyl chloride	760	28,731	84,504	642	20,281	35,492
Polypropylene	—	259	10,094	2,847	2,329	10,353
SBR, SBR Latex	270	810	5,128	810	810	19,430
Acrylic Fibers	—	—	50,317	—	50,317	—
Methanol	648	70,045	24,645	3,891	648	29,834

*Only Colombia produces caprolactam and there are no imports. It is assumed that Colombia supplies the market.
+The demands for Chile may be biased down by the abnormal economic conditions reigning in 1974.

73

of the degree of aggregation. Therefore Andean Common Market countries' imports were taken to be given by U.S. exports, for which highly disaggregated data are available.[5] The assumption that the U.S. is the sole supplier of the ACM countries is rational because of several reasons. First, the U.S. is the most advanced country in the production of petrochemicals. Second, the prices for products as listed in the U.S. were generally lower than in European countries. Third, the U.S. is the closest to the Andean Common Market and therefore transportation costs would offer an advantage. Lastly, it was found that among the relevant products the U.S. often exported to those countries that could have been considered the sources of ACM imports.

The total demands for the various products in the ACM were taken to grow at a rate of 11.4 percent per year. This rate of growth was estimated by the Junta del Acuerdo de Cartagena[6] and although optimistic it is in the range of the growth rates for petrochemical products in the U.S. and Europe.

The demands for the products of the petrochemical program in the member countries in 1985 are presented in Table 5.01.

IV

The demands for the various products in the member countries in 1985 were projected in the last section. The satisfaction of these demands with local production in 1985 will require the establishment of new plants. The purpose of this section is the calculation of the required investments for new plants.

In order to determine the required additional capacity for each industry in 1985, the available capacity was subtracted from the total required capacity which was taken to be 1.25 times larger than the total demand. The choice of the 1.25 coefficient is in accordance with an 80 percent capacity utilization assumption. This assumption was made because it was earlier assumed that it was the capacity utilization in 1974 and because such an assumption regarding capacity utilization would provide a margin for error in case the demands in 1985 should have been underestimated or the 1974 capacities should have become obsolete.

The necessary additional capacities and the accompanying investment requirements are presented in Table 5.02. The investment costs for the new plants were determined from data supplied in Hahn's *The Petrochemical Industry: Market and Economics* and from the investment costs of similar plants built in the past five years as reported in the *European Chemical News*.

The investment requirement for each industry was taken to be the mean of the actualized and standardized investment costs of all similar plants for which

Table 5.02. Investment Requirements

Industry	Additional Capacity Requirement* Tons Per Year	Investment Cost Millions of Dollars
Carbon black	94,536	21.0
Sodium cyanide	9,760	2.0
Tri- and perchloroethylene	7,241	2.9
Isopropyl alcohol	32,498	6.7
Butanol	22,750	4.0
Ethylene glycol	34,751	11.3
Propylene glycol	21,588	8.5
Phenol	10.788	6.6
Methyl methacrylate	14,134	5.0
Phthalic anhydride	18,916	9.1
Dimethyl terephthalate	91,374	45.0
Ethanolamines	4,025	2.7
2-4 Tolylene dissocyanate	7,902	18.0
Caprolactam	40,941	40.2
Polyethylene	242,916	29.5
Polystyrene	32,441	25.4
ABS, SAN resins	3,225	6.6
Polyvinyl chloride	242,734	41.0
Polypropylene	32,354	39.9
SBR, SBR Latex	33,734	12.0
Acrylic fibers	89,792	111.4
Methanol	162,141	18.8
		467.6

*Based on 1985 capacity requirements.

cost estimates were given. However, in a number of cases the median was taken to be the more representative figure.

The costs of plants as given in Hahn for 1965 and in the *European Chemical News* for the years 1970 to 1975 were indexed to 1975 with the use of the *Marshall and Stevens Equipment Index*. This index is regularly reported in the magazine *Chemical Engineering* and the entries for selected years are listed below.

Year	Index Value
1926	100.0
1965	245.0

1970	303.3
1971	321.3
1972	332.0
1973	344.1
1974	398.4
1975	444.3

The capital costs for different sized plants were standardized by using the formula:

$$\left[\frac{\text{cost of required plant}}{\text{cost of known plant}} \right] = \left[\frac{\text{capacity of required plant}}{\text{capacity of known plant}} \right]^{0.6}$$

Although the accuracy of the empirically determined 0.6 scale-up factor is the subject of some controversy,[7] it remains the quickest method for scaling plants up or down. Investment costs are not directly proportional to capacity requirements because, even though the reactor costs increase directly with capacity, there are economies of scale in purification, piping, and storage and the instrumentation and engineering costs remain basically constant.

V

In the calculation of DRCs it is important to subtract from both the domestic value added and the international value added, such payments as are made to foreign factors, and the payments or rental on imported capital. Although the correction for such payments could be complicated, it can be simplified if it is realized that the imported capital usually represents the foreign owned factor of production. This empirically apparent simplification does not introduce great errors because of the small impact that capital costs have on the actual DRC figures.

In most less developed countries where capital is a scarce factor the foreign owned factors of production often account for more than just imported capital. Since imported capital is included as a foreign factor of production, the term for the direct contribution of imported capital can be removed in order to avoid double counting if the foreign owned component is at least as large as the imported capital fraction.

In the actual calculations of DRCs it will be assumed that the foreign ownership is equal to the necessary imported capital. The imported component of the necessary investments was estimated by the Junta del Acuerdo de Cartagena to be 40 percent.[8] It is reasonable to set foreign ownership at 40 percent because according to the Cartagena Agreement foreign ownership could not exceed 49 percent if the industry was to benefit from the expanded market.

Having established a reasonable foreign ownership fraction it is then necessary to determine the rate of return expected by foreign investors. The quest for such a figure does, however, not lead to any results, as no writers will compromise themselves in quoting such an unknown quantity. Therefore, the only solution is to guess at such a figure, and here it was taken that the rate of return to foreign investors was 30 percent per year.

However, the rather arbitrary choices of a rate of return to foreign investors and their participation in the initial investment do not seriously distort the industry allocations. This results because the capital charges are subtracted from both the domestic value added in the numerator and the international value added in the denominator and therefore do not very much affect the estimates of the DRCs for the various industries in the various countries.[9]

The indirect contributions of imported capital and foreign owned factors of production would be even more difficult to determine and the effort would not be compensated, as the effect of these contributions would require very detailed input-output tables for all countries in addition to estimates respecting the share of imported capital and the rate of return to foreign investment. Given that these contributions would be subtracted from both the numerator and denominator in the estimation of DRCs, it is expected that their influence would be minimal at worst.

VI

The calculations of the DRCs can be simplified by treating imported capital as the imported factor of production. The computations can be further simplified by assuming the indirect contributions to value added attributable to imported capital and foreign factors of production to be zero. This assumption does not affect the results adversely because of the already mentioned insensitivity of the model to imported capital and foreign factors charges: the indirect contributions of imported capital and foreign factors are subtracted from both numerator and denominator in the calculation of the DRC for each industry in each country. Therefore the relationship between the DRCs for the various industries in the various countries remains constant within a reasonable margin of error.[10] The indirect contributions to value added attributable to tradable inputs can also be discounted in a similar manner since it is expected that on the average the contributions attributable to tradable inputs are similar in the various industries in the various countries. Therefore, given an initial assumption of zero transportation costs, the DRCs need no longer be calculated from equation **26** in Chapter III and can be calculated from:

$$
x_i^k = \frac{P_i(1 + t_i^k) - \sum_{g=G_i^k+1}^{H_i} a_{gi} P_g (1 + t_g^k) - v_{fi} s_f}{P_i - \sum_{g=G_i^k+1}^{H_i} a_{gi} P_g - v_{fi} s_f}
\tag{1}
$$

where:

x_i^k is the domestic resource cost of a unit of foreign exchange earned or saved in industry i in country k.

P_i is the international price of good i.

P_g is the international price of good g.

t_i^k is the tariff on good i in country k.

t_g^k is the tariff on good g in country k.

a_{gi} is the amount of input g necessary for the production of one unit of good i in physical units.

v_{fi} is the amount of foreign capital employed in the production of input good g.

s_f is the repatriated return to foreign capital.

$g = G_i^k+1, \ldots, H_i$ represent the imported inputs.

The estimation of the domestic resource cost of each industry in each country is presented in Table 5.03.

VII

The DRCs for all industries for all countries, assuming that transport costs of final products are zero, were presented in the last section. The purpose of this section is to determine the transport costs applicable to each industry in each of the member countries to compute a new set of DRCs that include transportation costs.

The estimation of transport costs is limited to the estimation of maritime freight costs between the ports of the member countries.[11] This simplification is made because inland transportation costs would depend on the particular locations within the countries. Although theoretically the model can be employed to allocate industries given several alternative locations per industry per country,

Table 5.03. Domestic Resource Costs of Foreign Exchange (transport costs assumed to be zero)

Industry	Bolivia	Chile	Colombia	Ecuador	Peru	Venezuela
Carbon black	1.41	1.23	1.17	1.12	1.42	1.47
Sodium cyanide	1.30	1.26	1.08	0.84	1.26	–*
Tri- and Perchloroethylene	1.43	1.80	0.91	1.09	1.05	0.88
Isopropanol	1.10	1.57	2.30	1.46	1.63	8.25
Butanol	1.26	1.07	1.26	1.00	1.75	1.10
Ethylene glycol	1.23	1.53	1.06	1.29	1.59	1.96
Propylene glycol	1.25	1.31	1.44	1.23	1.58	1.76
Phenol	1.17	1.44	1.28	1.15	1.55	1.39
Methyl methacrylate	1.22	1.21	1.17	1.13	1.48	1.39
Phthalic anhydride	1.29	1.06	1.41	1.00	1.57	2.46
Dimethyl terephthalate	1.29	1.88	1.00	0.98	1.94	2.84
Ethanolamines	1.23	1.42	0.88	1.03	1.77	–*
2-4 Tolylene dissocyanide	1.55	2.24	1.30	1.00	1.69	0.98
Caprolactam	1.64	1.67	2.17	0.77	1.02	1.42
Polyethylene	1.13	1.35	1.04	1.21	1.58	2.00
Polystyrenes	1.26	1.94	1.75	1.37	1.60	2.22
ABS, SAN Resins	1.64	1.84	1.31	1.88	2.43	3.68
Polyvinyl chloride	1.28	1.38	1.06	1.30	1.48	1.81
Polypropylene	1.54	1.78	1.40	1.99	2.50	4.31
SBR, SBR Latex	1.48	1.44	1.06	1.46	1.90	1.00
Acrylic Fibers	1.26	1.41	1.12	1.44	1.50	2.84
Methanol	1.28	1.23	1.18	1.12	2.01	1.29

*Impossible to calculate a meaningful value for this entry. The values computed were too small to be credible.

such an approach would very much complicate the computational aspects of the industry allocations.

Transportation costs are very difficult to determine and the estimates of these costs must be taken as approximate. There are two reasons for the estimation of transport cost difficulties. The first is that there is very little trade between some of the member countries and therefore the amount of data is very limited. Second, the data available on rates are not necessarily indicative of costs since these rates are set by conferences, which are formal agreements between the shipping companies with respect to rates. In addition sometimes these conference rates are confidential.[12]

The United Nations' Economic Commission for Latin America studied maritime freight rates in 1965.[13] One of the fundamental discoveries of this study was that freight rates for different products on the same route were determined by the value of the products and by their stowage factor. This result can be interpreted to mean that the stowage factor basically determines the cost of transportation. Surcharges are made to this basic cost on the basis of the per volume price of the product that determines "what the market can bear."[14]

Therefore it was assumed that the transportation costs for any petrochemical product between two countries was given by the average of the transportation costs of low value per volume commodities. Assignment of different transportation costs to different petrochemical products on the same route because of stowage factor differences was not attempted because of their relatively minor importance.

The transportation cost figures obtained from the United Nations' study were for 1965. Since then, because of the increases in the prices of petroleum and of equipment, transportation costs have increased sharply. The transportation cost figures were indexed to 1975 with the transportation cost index published in the *Survey of Current Business* of the U.S. Department of Commerce.[15] Although this index refers to transportation in the U.S., it was taken to be adaptable to freight rates since increases in the cost of petroleum products and equipment are common to both.

The transportation costs per ton between any pair of countries are given in Table 5.04.

VIII

The new DRCs, including transport costs, are calculated from the DRCs of Section VII by adding to the domestic value added in the numerator the cost of transporting the products to the countries where the demand is. That is, a transportation cost element is added to the numerator of the DRC equation presented

Table 5.04.   Transport Costs in Dollars per Ton*

	Bolivia	Chile	Colombia	Ecuador	Peru	Venezuela
Bolivia	0.0	22.5	33.8	27.9	25.2	66.8
Chile	22.5	0.0	30.2	22.0	23.0	44.0
Colombia	33.8	31.4	0.0	24.9	36.2	41.7
Ecuador	27.9	24.4	24.4	0.0	31.4	37.7
Peru	25.2	25.2	31.4	31.4	0.0	37.7
Venezuela	66.8	70.7	46.4	58.2	62.9	0.0

*Note that the entries for the transport costs between the two countries are asymmetric reflecting mainly the differences in load factors.

in Section VII for each industry for each country. The transportation cost element is given by the sum of the products of the fractional or per ton demands of the countries and the transportation costs from the supplying country (equation 28 of Chapter III). It is expected that as a result of the inclusion of transportation costs those countries with a great share of the demand for a product from a given industry will be somewhat favored in the assignment of that industry.

The DRCs calculated including transport costs are presented in Table 5.05.

IX

In this chapter the data required for the implementation of the model were discussed. The purpose of this section is to present a general evaluation of the data and specify the limitations imposed on the model.

The main components of the data framework are: input coefficients, prices, tariffs, capital costs, and transport costs. The physical input coefficients obtained were empirically determined or calculated on the basis of the necessary chemical reactions and therefore present a reliable set of data to serve as a basis for further calculations. The data on prices and tariffs, although not as reliable as that for input coefficients, are also well founded. The determination of capital and transport costs was, however, somewhat less rigorous because of the lack of adequate data.

The lack of precise data on investment requirements and, therefore, capital costs has very little influence on the DRCs. Thus, the fact that the data on capital costs are not very precise does not cause any problems.

The lack of precision in the estimation of transport costs is more serious even though the estimates of transportation costs are more reliable than those for capital costs. This results from the fact that transportation costs do affect the

Table 5.05. Domestic Resource Cost of Foreign Exchange — Transport Included

Industry	Bolivia	Chile	Colombia	Ecuador	Peru	Venezuela
Carbon black	1.64	1.40	1.25	1.27	1.59	1.62
Sodium cyanide	1.48	1.30	1.24	0.98	1.37	—*
Tri- and Perchloroethylene	1.59	1.92	0.96	1.20	1.18	1.08
Isopropanol	2.30	2.41	2.99	2.17	2.36	8.54
Butanol	1.43	1.14	1.42	1.14	1.88	1.38
Ethylene glycol	1.40	1.66	1.13	1.40	1.71	2.08
Propylene glycol	1.40	1.41	1.53	1.32	1.68	1.84
Phenol	1.31	1.55	1.32	1.24	1.65	1.48
Methyl methacrylate	1.39	1.33	1.27	1.24	1.59	1.48
Phthalic anhydride	1.48	1.18	1.52	1.12	1.69	2.55
Dimethyl terephthalate	1.44	1.96	1.09	1.09	2.06	3.05
Ethanolamine	1.72	1.78	1.14	1.33	2.08	—*
2-4 Tolylene diisocyanate	1.73	2.36	1.42	1.10	1.80	1.05
Caprolactam	1.74	1.76	2.17	0.84	1.11	1.55
Polyethylene	1.23	1.41	1.10	1.28	1.66	2.14
Polystyrene	1.37	2.01	1.83	1.45	1.68	2.38
ABS, SAN Resins	1.85	2.00	1.43	2.02	2.58	3.88
Polyvinyl chloride	1.36	1.44	1.10	1.36	1.54	1.90
Polypropylene	1.92	2.06	1.60	2.22	2.76	4.57
SBR, SBR Latex	1.67	1.57	1.16	1.57	2.02	1.05
Acrylic Fibers	1.26	1.41	1.12	1.44	1.50	2.84
Methanol	1.64	1.40	1.46	1.39	2.30	1.78

*Impossible to calculate a meaningful value for this entry. The values computed were too small to be credible.

DRCs. In order to minimize distortions in the allocations of industries, transport costs for all products on the same routes were taken to be equal. Although this simplification is expected to minimize any distortions caused by errors in the estimates of transportation costs, it precludes analysis of the sensitivities of the allocations to changes in the transport costs of particular goods on particular routes. Sensitivity analyses can only be done for either general increases in transportation costs or increases in the costs along one route. These analyses will be partially performed in the next chapter where the allocations of industries based on DRCs excluding and including transport costs will be compared.

The reliability of the other data on inputs, prices, and tariffs permit an adequate assessment of comparative advantages. Sensitivity analyses with respect to domestic prices will indicate the price ranges within which particular countries will maintain comparative advantages. Further, if in particular industries no country presents a comparative advantage it can be concluded that no country has a comparative advantage, rather than that errors distorted the advantages.

6 ALLOCATIONS OF INDUSTRIES GIVEN NUMERICAL DISTRIBUTIONAL CONSTRAINTS

The present chapter and the next are devoted to analyses of industry allocations given different distributional constraints. These analyses are divided into two chapters because different computational techniques can be employed in the implementation of the model depending on the types of distributional constraints. In this chapter industry allocations determined with a linear programming routine will be analyzed. Industry allocations determined with an integer program will be examined in the next chapter.

In the first section of this chapter the requirements for the implementation of the model with a linear programming routine are discussed. The model can be implemented using a linear program to determine industry allocations only if the distributional constraints are of the type that establish the number of industries to be assigned to each country.

In the second section the advantages and limitations of the use of linear programming routines are described. The relevance of numerical distributional constraints is analyzed and suggestions are made for the utilization of such constraints to simulate other types of constraints if integer programming routines are not available.

The third section is devoted to the comparison of allocations determined using DRCs computed excluding and including transport costs and subject to numerical income- and population-based constraints. These comparisons are made to establish the importance of transportation costs. Also, these comparisons will determine the degree of confidence to be placed on allocations based on DRCs computed including transportation costs.

In the fourth section the industry allocations constrained by distributional requirements based on either income or population are compared. The allocations of particular industries to given countries are analyzed. The sensitivity of the allocations to changes in production costs is also examined.

Different allocations of industries imply different costs for supplying the common market with a given amount of goods. Given alternative allocations of industries, the costs of supplying the area with the products of the petro-chemical industries will be investigated in Section V.

In Section VI the applicability of the results obtained by allocating industries with a linear program is investigated. The significance of the actual allocations and their usefulness as a basis for further negotiations are examined.

I

Transportation problems are a special class of linear programming problems. Transportation problems are differentiated from other linear programming problems in that they are concerned with the selection of distribution routes between suppliers and consumers, or suppliers, any number of storage or processing stages, and consumers. The classical transportation problem is usually formulated to determine how much each of several plants should produce and how much of this production each plant should ship to each distribution center. It is usually assumed that production costs per unit are equal at all sources and that therefore the problem is limited to the selection of a distribution pattern that minimizes transport costs.

The general formulation for an m-plant n-consumer or distribution center model is:

$$\text{Minimize} \sum_{i=1}^{m} \sum_{j=1}^{n} d_{ij} y_{ij} \tag{1}$$

subject to

$$\sum_{j=1}^{n} y_{ij} \leqslant S_i \quad i = 1 \ldots m \text{ (supply)} \tag{2}$$

$$\sum_{i=1}^{m} y_{ij} \geq D_j \quad j = 1 \ldots n \text{ (demand)} \tag{3}$$

where

d_{ij} stands for the transportation cost per unit for items produced at plant i and shipped to center j.

y_{ij} is the amount of the product of plant i shipped to point j. That is, the y_{ij}s are the variables to be determined.

S_i represents the supply capacity of plant i.

D_j represents the demand of the consumer or distribution center j.

The general information of the transportation model is strikingly similar to that of the model designed to allocate industries. The objective function of the allocation model is given by equation 14 of Chapter IV as:

$$\text{Minimize} \sum_{i=1}^{n} \sum_{k=1}^{m} (x_i^k + c_i^k) \frac{W_i}{W_t} Z_i^k \tag{4}$$

where

x_i^k is the domestic resource cost of foreign exchange in industry i in country k.

c_i^k is the per unit transportation cost of delivering the products of industry i in country k to the various markets.

W_i is the total international value added in industry i.

W_t is the total international value added of all the assignable industries.

Z_i^k is a dichotomous variable that takes on the value of one if the ith industry is assigned to country k and zero otherwise.

The objective of the optimization function (equation 4) is the minimization of the production and distribution costs per unit of value added in the industries assigned to the various countries. This objective is similar to that of the transportation problem since the d_{ij}s can be formulated to comprise both production and transportation costs.

The minimization function of the two models differs in that the variables to be determined are different except in special cases. The decision variables of the transportation model are real numbers that can assume any positive values. The Z_i^ks of the allocation model are integers limited to the values of 0 and 1. The decision variables of the transportation problem will, however, be limited to the values of 0 and 1 if the constraints of the transportation model are such that the coefficients of the y_{ij}s in the constraints are all 0 or 1, the right-hand sides of the "smaller or equal to" constraints are all 0 and 1, and the right-hand side values of the "greater than or equal to" constraints are integers.

The restrictions on the constraints necessary for a binary solution to the allocation problem are similar to the restrictions on the constraints of the assignment problem. The assignment problem is a special case of the transportation problem. The distinguishing features of the assignment problem is that the objective is the minimization of the cost[1] of assigning jobs or workers to plants or machines. The typical assignment problem for assigning n jobs to m plants is written:

$$\text{Minimize} \sum_{i=1}^{n} \sum_{j=1}^{m} d_{ij} y_{ij} \tag{5}$$

subject to

$$\sum_{j=1}^{m} y_{ij} \leqslant 1 \qquad i = 1 \ldots n \tag{6}$$

$$\sum_{i=1}^{n} y_{ij} = 1 \qquad j = 1 \ldots m \tag{7}$$

where

d_{ij} represents the cost of assigning job i to plant j.
y_{ij} is the dichotomous variable that determines whether job i is assigned to plant j or not.

The objective function states that the cost of assigning jobs $i = 1 \ldots n$ to plants $j = 1 \ldots m$ should be minimized. The first set of constraints ensures that specific jobs are not assigned to more than one plant. The second set of constraints ensures that all plants receive a project. There is a feasible solution if the number of jobs n is "equal to or greater than" the number of plants m.

The assignment problem is a special form of zero-one integer programming that can be solved with a linear program because of the nature of the constraints. The constraints in an assignment problem have as coefficients for the decision variables and as right-hand sides only zeroes and ones. These zeroes and ones determine the extreme points of the feasible region. Since the optimal solution to a linear program lies at an extreme point, the decision variables can only assume values of zero and one.

The purpose of the allocation model developed in Chapter IV is to assign a number of industries n to a number of countries m. The restrictions on the industry allocations are that any one industry should not be allocated to more than one country and that the industry allocations should conform to certain distributional considerations. The first restriction, that no industry i be assigned to more than one country k, can be formulated as:

$$\sum_{k=1}^{m} Z_i^k \leqslant 1 \qquad \text{for all industries } i = 1 \ldots n \qquad (8)$$

This set of supply restrictions is identical to that of the assignment problem and therefore does not affect the obtainment of 0,1 solutions with a linear program.

The allocation model can be implemented with a linear programming routine if the coefficients of the decision variables in the distributional constraints are zeroes and ones and the right-hand sides of these constraints are integers. The right-hand sides need not be zeroes and ones as required by the assignment problem because the solutions to the transportation model will be integer numbers if the right-hand sides are integer numbers.[2] The supply constraints of the allocation model limit the values that the decision variables may assume to zero and one. Therefore, it is possible to assign more than one industry to any one country. The distributional constraints for the allocation model are formulated as:

$$\sum_{i=1}^{n} Z_i^k \geqslant n \qquad \text{for all countries } k = 1 \ldots m \qquad (9)$$

where n is a positive integer. The industry allocation model given by equations 4, 8, and 9 can therefore be solved with linear programming techniques.

II

In the last section it was pointed out that linear programming methods were applicable to the solving of the allocation problem if the constraints to the allocation problem meet certain conditions. In this section the advantages of the applicability of linear programming methods in comparison with integer programming methods will first be analyzed. Second, the limitations imposed on the model by the restrictions on the constraints will be examined.

Linear programming problems are customarily solved with the simplex algorithm, a solution procedure that yields optimal solutions in a small number of steps. The solution methods for integer programming problems are generally based on enumeration procedures that examine large numbers of feasible solutions in the determination of optimal solutions. Linear programming problems are much easier to solve than integer programming problems because of the efficiency of the simplex algorithm as compared to enumeration algorithms. Because linear programming problems are easier to solve, it is advantageous to implement the allocation model as a linear program whenever possible: the determination of an optimal solution with a linear programming routine is computationally easier than with an integer programming routine and therefore less costly in terms of computer time.

The implementation of the model as a linear programming problem is also advantageous because the solution procedure generates information that is useful in the estimation of the sensitivity of the solution. The nature of the simplex algorithm is such that in the computation of the primal solution, the dual is also determined. Given the primal and dual solutions, the sensitivity of the optimal solution to changes in the coefficients of the objective function and to changes in the right-hand side values of the constraints is easily determined; most linear programming computer codes not only list the primal and dual solutions but also present data on the sensitivity of the optimal solution. The sensitivity of the optimal solution of an integer program must be empirically determined.

Linear programming solution methods can be applied to binary integer programming problems only if the constraints of these problems obey certain restrictions. The limitations imposed by the restrictions on the constraints dictate the usefulness of linear programming routines for solving allocation of industries problems. As pointed out in the last section, the restrictions on the constraints are that the coefficients of the decision variables have values of zero or one, that the right-hand sides of the "smaller than or equal to" constraints be equal to one, and that the right-hand sides of the "greater than or equal to" constraints be integer numbers. These restrictions limit the use of linear programming routines to allocation problems where the distributional constraints determine the number of industries to be allocated to each country. Distributional constraints based on numbers of industries are relevant only if the desired characteristics of the industries are similar. Numerical constraints are useful if the industries are generally of the same size as measured by either gross sales, value added in production or investment requirements. If the industries to be allocated are of very different sizes, allocations according to numbers of industries are probably not significant. The required simplicity of the constraints thus imposes an important limitation on the usefulness of linear programming routines for allocating industries.

Given industries of different sizes, the numerical distribution constraint limitations could be somewhat removed by redefining the problem so that allocations could still be made with linear programming routines. The smallest industry to be allocated could serve as a common denominator and the large industries could be divided so as to provide a set of industries of equal size. These could then be distributed with a linear program with numerical constraints. However, the problem with such a scheme would be that although most of the time all the subdivisions of an industry would be assigned to one country, this would not necessarily be the case and industries could be split up. Furthermore, the data on the sensitivity of the solution to changes in the cost coefficients or the right-hand sides would not be meaningful.

III

The purpose of this section is to compare allocations of industries based on DRCs computed excluding and including transport costs. These comparisons serve to establish whether production costs or transportation costs are the more important in the determination of plant locations. Also, since the transport cost figures are not precise, the results of the analysis of this section will determine the reliability of allocations based on DRCs that include transport costs.

The number of industries assigned any one country was the rounded value of the product of the country's share of income or population and the number of industries to be allocated. However, at least one industry was assigned each country regardless of the rounded value of the product. The incomes and populations of the countries are presented in Table 6.01. In Table 6.02 the number of

Table 6.01.   The Incomes and Populations of the Member Countries

Country	Income* (Million Dollars Per Year)	Population[†] (Million)
Bolivia	1,265	5.63
Chile	8,725	10.25
Colombia	8,750	23.63
Ecuador	2,085	6.73
Peru	7,629	15.87
Venezuela	13,519	11.99

*The 1974 income was taken to be equal to the 1974 GDP at 1970 prices divided by the average 1970 exchange rate as given in the International Monetary Fund's *International Financial Statistics,* XXX (January 1977). The 1970 prices were chosen to minimize the distortion in the calculation of Chile's national income, since Chile was undergoing rapid inflation in 1974.

[†]*Source:* United Nations *Monthly Bulletin of Statistics,* August, 1976 (6), p. 1.

Table 6.02. The Number of Industries Assigned Each of the Member Countries on the Basis of Either Income or Population

Country	Number Based on Income	Number Based on Population
Bolivia	1	2
Chile	4	3
Colombia	5	7
Ecuador	1	2
Peru	4	5
Venezuela	7	3

industries to be assigned to each country on the basis of either income or population is presented.

Based on DRCs computed excluding and including transportation costs, the allocations of industries constrained by income distributional requirements are presented in Tables 6.03 and 6.04. The sensitivity of the solution to changes in the coefficients of the decision variables is indicated by the range between the weighted domestic resource cost of production for an industry in a given country and the maximum cost of production for the same industry to be assigned to the same country. That is, for any one industry this range indicates the amount by which costs could increase in the country with the assignment, before this cost increase affected the industry allocation.

An examination of Tables 6.03 and 6.04 indicates that only five industries out of 22 change location with the introduction of transportation costs. Some location changes are caused by changes in the relative values of the DRCs, due to the introduction of transportation costs; these changes in turn induce further changes as industries have to be reallocated so as to satisfy the distributional constraints. The demand for carbon black is concentrated in Colombia and Venezuela and, therefore, the introduction of transport costs caused this industry to be reallocated away from Chile to Colombia. Chile, who demonstrates the greatest demand for methanol, was compensated by the reassignment of methanol away from Venezuela in favor of Chile. In order to satisfy the distributional requirements Venezuela was assigned the tri- and perchloroethylene industry, which was taken away from Peru. Peru in turn was assigned the caprolactam industry, which was taken away from Ecuador. The circle was completed by assigning Ecuador the dimethyl terephthalate industry, which was taken away from Colombia.

The limited number of changes in the allocation of industries, due to the introduction of transport costs, indicates that the industry allocations are not very

Table 6.03. Industry Allocation Given Income-Based Numerical Constraints and DRCs Computed Excluding Transport Costs

Industry	Country	Weighted DRC $(\times 10^4)$	Upper Bound for Weighted DRC $(\times 10^4)$	Percent Difference
Carbon black	Chile	449.	456.	1.6
Sodium cyanide	Peru	45.	71.	57.8
Tri- and Perchloro-ethylene	Peru	33.	34.	3.0
Isopropanol	Peru	49.	73.	49.0
Butanol	Venezuela	92.	109.	18.5
Ethylene glycol	Colombia	184.	222.	20.6
Propylene glycol	Chile	179.	190.	6.1
Phenol	Venezuela	92.	95.	3.3
Methyl methacrylate	Venezuela	104.	105.	1.0
Phthalic anhydride	Chile	87.	103.	18.4
Dimethyl terephthalate	Colombia	413.	544.	31.7
Ethanolamines	Peru	14.	37.	164.3
2-4 Tolylene diisocyanate	Venezuela	43.	67.	55.8
Caprolactam	Ecuador	212.	370.	74.5
Polyethylene	Colombia	1658.	1813.	9.3
Polystyrene	Bolivia	247.	270.	9.3
ABS, SAN Resins	Venezuela	12.	16.	33.3
Polyvinyl chloride	Colombia	2207.	2677.	21.3
Polypropylene	Chile	134.	157.	17.2
SBR, SBR Latex	Venezuela	192.	252.	31.2
Acrylic Fibers	Colombia	4168.	4702.	12.8
Methanol	Venezuela	400.	411.	2.8
Total		11,014.		

sensitive to transport costs. Although transport costs are significant the industry allocations are not very sensitive to transportation costs because the product demands are generally evenly distributed among the countries. The implications of this insensitivity to transport costs are that the production costs are the main determinants of industry allocations and that the effect of small errors in the estimation of transport costs on industry allocations is small.

Tables 6.05 and 6.06 present the allocations of industries obtained, given constraints based on population. The allocation of industries presented in Table

Table 6.04. Industry Allocation Given Income-Based Numerical Constraints and DRCs Computed Including Transport Costs

Industry	Country	Weighted DRC ($\times 10^4$)	Upper Bound for Weighted DRC ($\times 10^4$)	Percent Difference
Carbon black	Colombia	456.	464.	1.8
Sodium cyanide	Peru	49.	84.	71.4
Tri- and Perchloro-ethylene	Venezuela	34.	59.	73.5
Isopropanol	Peru	71.	109.	53.5
Butanol	Venezuela	116.	155.	33.6
Ethylene glycol	Colombia	197.	224.	13.7
Propylene glycol	Chile	193.	311.	61.1
Phenol	Venezuela	98.	131.	33.7
Methyl methacrylate	Venezuela	111.	141.	27.0
Phthalic anhydride	Chile	97.	102.	5.2
Dimethyl terephtha-late	Ecuador	450.	458.	1.8
Ethanolamines	Peru	17.	51.	200.0
2-4 Tolylene diisocyanate	Venezuela	46.	101.	120.0
Caprolactam	Peru	306.	324.	5.9
Polyethylene	Colombia	1753.	1947.	11.1
Polystyrene	Bolivia	268.	282.	5.2
ABS, SAN Resins	Venezuela	47.	53.	12.8
Polyvinyl chloride	Colombia	2290.	2819.	23.1
Polypropylene	Chile	154.	157.	1.9
SBR, SBR Latex	Venezuela	202.	319.	57.9
Acrylic Fibers	Colombia	4169.	4677.	12.2
Methanol	Chile	434.	468.	7.8
Total		11,558.		

6.05 was obtained on the basis of DRCs computed excluding transport costs and that presented in Table 6.06 was obtained on the basis of DRCs computed including transport costs. The investigation of the influence of transport costs was repeated for the case of population constrained allocations because distributional constraints affect the sensitivity of allocations to changes in the coefficients of the decision variables.

Although the industry allocations presented in Tables 6.05 and 6.06 are much more sensitive to changes in the cost coefficients than the allocations of Tables

Table 6.05. Industry Allocation Given Population-Based Numerical Constraints and DRCs Computed Excluding Transport Costs

Industry	Country	Weighted DRC ($\times 10^4$)	Upper Bound for Weighted DRC ($\times 10^4$)	Percent Difference
Carbon black	Colombia	427.	428.	0.2
Sodium cyanide	Peru	45.	62.	37.8
Tri- and Perchloro-ethylene	Peru	33.	42.	27.3
Isopropanol	Peru	49.	58.	18.4
Butanol	Venezuela	92.	96.	4.3
Ethylene glycol	Colombia	184.	206.	12.0
Propylene glycol	Chile	179.	183.	2.2
Phenol	Bolivia	77.	81.	5.2
Methyl methacrylate	Chile	91.	94.	3.3
Phthalic anhydride	Chile	87.	112.	28.7
Dimethyl terephtha-late	Colombia	413.	423.	2.4
Ethanolamines	Peru	14.	28.	100.0
2-4 Tolylene diisocyanate	Venezuela	43.	59.	37.2
Caprolactam	Ecuador	212.	385.	81.6
Polyethylene	Colombia	1658.	1793.	8.1
Polystyrene	Bolivia	247.	289.	17.0
ABS, SAN Resins	Peru	23.	27.	17.4
Polyvinyl chloride	Colombia	2207.	2657.	20.4
Polypropylene	Colombia	105.	108.	2.8
SBR, SBR Latex	Venezuela	192.	222.	13.5
Acrylic Fibers	Colombia	4168.	4682.	12.3
Methanol	Ecuador	347.	348.	2.9
Total		10,893.		

6.03 and 6.04, as indicated by the "Percent Difference" columns, the effect of the introduction of transport costs is small. Four industries are exchanged due to the inclusion of transport costs: two changes caused by demand concentration induce two more changes. Chile demonstrates the greatest demand for methanol and is assigned the industry when transportation costs are included. Ecuador, which would have been assigned the methanol industry if transport costs were zero, is compensated by the assignment of the propylene glycol industry, which is taken away from Chile. Similarly, Chile and Venezuela exchange the butanol

Table 6.06. Industry Allocation Given Population-Based Numerical Constraints and DRCs Computed Including Transport Costs

Industry	Country	Weighted DRC $(\times 10^4)$	Upper Bound for Weighted DRC $(\times 10^4)$	Percent Difference
Carbon black	Colombia	456.	464.	1.8
Sodium cyanide	Peru	49.	61.	24.5
Tri- and Perchloro-ethylene	Peru	37.	42.	13.5
Isopropanol	Peru	71.	84.	18.3
Butanol	Chile	96.	105.	9.4
Ethylene glycol	Colombia	197.	233.	18.3
Propylene glycol	Ecuador	181.	186.	2.8
Phenol	Bolivia	86.	86.	0.0
Methyl methacrylate	Venezuela	111.	111.	0.0
Phthalic anhydride	Chile	97.	104.	7.2
Dimethyl Terephthalate	Colombia	450.	457.	1.6
Ethanolamines	Peru	17.	28.	64.7
2-4 Tolylene diisocyanate	Venezuela	46.	71.	54.3
Caprolactam	Ecuador	232.	280.	20.7
Polyethylene	Colombia	1753.	1949.	11.2
Polystyrene	Bolivia	268.	295.	10.1
ABS, SAN Resins	Peru	31.	37.	19.4
Polyvinyl chloride	Colombia	2290.	2821.	23.2
Polypropylene	Colombia	120.	133.	10.8
SBR, SBR Latex	Venezuela	202.	246.	21.8
Acrylic Fibers	Colombia	4169.	4679.	12.2
Methanol	Chile	434.	443.	2.1
Total		11,393.		

and methyl methacrylate industries: Chile has the greatest demand for butanol and is assigned the industry when transport costs are included. Venezuela, which would have received the industry in the absence of transportation costs, is compensated with the assignment of the methyl methacrylate industry.

A comparison of Tables 6.05 and 6.06 again indicates that production costs are the main determinants of industry allocations. Further, the conclusion respecting the relative unimportance of transportation costs, as revealed by the small number of industry reassignments caused by the introduction of transport costs, cannot be attributed to the nature of the constraints. In fact, as empirically determined, the nature of the distributional constraints is such that the sensitivity of the allocations to changes in the coefficients of the decision variables is fairly high: allocations derived with other types of constraints would not be as sensitive.

In the establishment of the relative unimportance of transportation costs as compared to production costs it was implied that industry allocations were not very sensitive to changes in transportation costs. The sensitivity of industry allocations to changes in transport costs will now be determined. The possible increase in the cost of transportation per ton in a given industry is given by the product of the difference between the upper bound for the weighted DRC and the weighted DRC and the total international value added in all industries divided by the number of tons of the specific product demanded in the whole market. That is, the permissible increase in transportation costs is given by the difference between the upper bound on the domestic value added per ton and the domestic value added per ton in the particular industry assigned to a specific country. The possible percentage increase in the transport costs is given by the transport cost increase divided by the transportation cost incurred in the shipment of the goods from the assigned production country to the locations of the demands. The possible changes in transport costs that would not affect the allocation of Table 6.04 are presented in Table 6.07.

Table 6.07. The Sensitivity of the Industry Allocation of Table 6.04 to General Increases in Transportation Costs (the Institutable Transportation Cost Increases That Would not Affect the Allocation)

Industry	Transport Cost (Dollars Per Ton)	Permissible Transport Cost Increase (Dollars Per Ton)	Permissible Percentage Increase
Carbon black	15.9	4.4	27.7
Sodium cyanide	20.8	186.7	898.0
Tri- and Perchloro- ethylene	44.7	179.7	402.0
Isopropanol	34.5	60.9	176.5
Butanol	54.1	89.2	164.9
Ethylene glycol	19.2	40.4	210.4
Propylene glycol	33.8	284.6	842.0
Phenol	30.6	159.2	520.2

Table 6.07. *Continued*

Industry	Transport Cost (Dollars Per Ton)	Permissible Transport Cost Increase (Dollars Per Ton)	Permissible Percentage Increase
Methyl methacrylate	27.2	110.5	406.2
Phthalic anhydride	33.7	13.8	40.9
Dimethyl terephthalate	26.7	4.6	17.2
Ethanolamines	32.2	439.8	1365.8
2-4 Tolylene Diisocyanate	21.7	362.3	1669.6
Caprolactam	31.1	22.9	73.6
Polyethylene	22.3	41.6	186.5
Polystyrene	33.4	22.5	67.4
ABS, SAN Resins	37.5	96.8	258.1
Polyvinyl chloride	18.4	113.4	616.3
Polypropylene	33.9	4.8	14.2
SBR, SBR Latex	15.2	180.6	1188.2
Acrylic Fibers	18.1	294.5	1627.0
Methanol	17.0	10.9	64.1

An examination of Table 6.07 indicates that transport costs in general can vary fairly widely without affecting the particular allocation presented in Table 6.04. Transport costs have to increase by large amounts before the particular allocation of Table 6.04 is affected because the allocations of industries are mainly determined by production costs. For any industry the permissible percentage increase in transport costs refers to increases in the costs along all routes: increases in the costs along one route could be several times larger and yet not affect the particular allocation. Therefore, small errors in the computation of transport costs are not expected to have very pronounced effects on the industry allocations.

The industry allocation presented in Table 6.06 is much more sensitive to changes in costs than the allocation of Table 6.04. Therefore, as presented in Table 6.08, the permissible transportation cost increases are smaller for the allocation of Table 6.06 than they are for the allocation of Table 6.04. However, in general, the conclusions previously delineated regarding the insensitivity of industry allocations to changes in transportation costs can also be derived from an analysis of the allocation of Table 6.06.

Table 6.08. The Sensitivity of the Industry Allocation of Table 6.06 to General Increases in Transportation Costs (the Institutable Transportation Cost Increase That Would not Affect the Allocation)

Industry	Transport Cost (Dollars Per Ton)	Permissible Transport Cost Increase (Dollars Per Ton)	Permissible Percentage Increase
Carbon black	29.4	4.4	15.0
Sodium cyanide	20.8	64.0	307.7
Tri- and Perchloro- ethylene	28.8	35.9	124.6
Isopropanol	34.5	20.8	60.3
Butanol	13.2	20.6	156.1
Ethylene glycol	19.2	53.9	280.7
Propylene glycol	30.6	12.0	39.2
Phenol	45.0	0.0	0.0
Methyl methacrylate	27.2	0.0	0.0
Phthalic anhydride	33.7	19.3	57.2
Dimethyl terephthalate	21.2	4.0	18.9
Ethanolamines	32.2	142.3	441.9
2-4 Tolylene diisocyanate	21.7	164.7	759.0
Caprolactam	24.4	61.0	250.0
Polyethylene	22.3	42.0	188.3
Polystyrene	33.4	43.3	129.6
ABS, SAN Resins	28.8	96.8	336.1
Polyvinyl chloride	18.4	113.9	519.0
Polypropylene	24.1	20.9	86.7
SBR, SBR Latex	15.2	67.9	446.7
Acrylic Fibers	18.1	295.7	1633.7
Methanol	17.0	2.9	17.1

IV

Distributional constraints expressed as the numbers of industries to be assigned to the various countries are most meaningful if the industries to be allocated are similar in size, which is taken to represent either the total sales value, the total value added, or the investment requirement. However, even if the industries are of different sizes, allocations subject to numerical constraints may be relevant if other concerns such as the adoption of new technologies are evident. Also, such allocations may be appropriate if the allocation is but a small part of a much larger program. Moreover, even if such industry allocations cannot be realistically implemented in practice, the analysis of such allocations can provide information regarding the countries' comparative cost advantages that can be very useful in subsequent negotiations.

As explained in Chapter IV, the relatively more developed countries would benefit most from a system of distribution based on the incomes of the countries. The relatively less developed countries would prefer a system of distribution based on population. An industry allocation constrained by income-based restrictions is presented in Table 6.09.[3] A similar allocation constrained by

Table 6.09. The Industries Assigned to the Member Countries Given Numerical Income Constraints

Country	Industry	Weighted DRC $(\times 10^4)$	Upper Bound for Weighted DRC $(\times 10^4)$	Percent Difference
Bolivia	Polystyrene	268.	282.	5.2
Chile	Propylene glycol	193.	311.	61.1
	Phthalic anhydride	97.	102.	5.2
	Polypropylene	154.	157.	1.9
	Methanol	434.	468.	7.8
Colombia	Carbon black	456.	464.	1.8
	Ethylene glycol	197.	224.	13.7
	Polyethylene	1753.	1947.	11.1
	Polyvinyl chloride	2290.	2819.	23.1
	Acrylic fibers	4169.	4677.	12.2
Ecuador	Dimethyl terephthalate	450.	458.	1.8
Peru	Sodium cyanide	49.	84.	71.4
	Isopropanol	71.	109.	53.5
	Ethanolamines	17.	51.	200.0
	Caprolactam	306.	324.	5.9
Venezuela	Tri- and Perchloroethylene	34.	59.	73.5
	Butanol	116.	155.	33.6
	Phenol	98.	131.	33.7
	Methyl methacrylate	111.	141.	27.0
	2-4 Tolylene diisocyanate	46.	101.	120.0
	ABS, SAN Resins	47.	53.	12.8
	SBR, SBR Latex	202.	319.	57.9

population-based restrictions is presented in Table 6.10. Tables 6.09 and 6.10 were derived from Tables 6.04 and 6.06, respectively.

A comparison of Tables 6.09 and 6.10 reveals which industries are reassigned when population distributional constraints are substituted for income distributional constraints. Table 6.09 presents the minimum acceptable number of industries for the countries with the relatively smaller incomes per capita: Bolivia, Ecuador, Colombia, and Peru. Table 6.10 presents the minimum demands of the relatively richer Venezuela and Chile.

Table 6.10. The Industries Assigned to the Member Countries Given Numerical Population Constraints

Country	Industry	Weighted DRC $(\times 10^4)$	Upper Bound for Weighted DRC $(\times 10^4)$	Percent Difference
Bolivia	Phenol	86.	86.	0.0
	Polystyrene	268.	295.	10.1
Chile	Butanol	96.	105.	9.4
	Phthalic anhydride	97.	104.	7.2
	Methanol	434.	443.	2.1
Colombia	Carbon black	456.	464.	1.8
	Ethylene glycol	197.	233.	18.3
	Dimethyl terephthalate	450.	457.	1.6
	Polyethylene	1753.	1949.	11.2
	Polyvinyl chloride	2290.	2821.	23.2
	Polypropylene	120.	133.	10.8
	Acrylic Fibers	4169.	4679.	12.2
Ecuador	Propylene glycol	181.	186.	2.8
	Caprolactam	232.	280.	20.7
Peru	Sodium cyanide	49.	61.	24.5
	Tri- and Perchloroethylene	37.	42.	13.5
	Isopropanol	71.	84.	18.3
	Ethanolamines	17.	28.	64.7
	ABS, SAN Resins	31.	37.	19.4
Venezuela	Methyl methacrylate	111.	111.	0.0
	2-4 Tolylene diisocyanate	46.	71.	54.3
	SBR, SBR Latex	202.	246.	21.8

Given income distributional constraints, the polystyrene industry is assigned to Bolivia. Bolivia is one of the relatively poorer countries and is assigned more industries in a population-based allocation. A distribution based on population awards Bolivia two industries. Therefore in addition to the polystyrene industry Bolivia is assigned the phenol industry that is taken away from Venezuela. Venezuela is awarded the phenol industry if the distribution is based on income.

Ecuador is assigned the dimethyl terephthalate industry if the distribution is made according to income and Ecuador is to receive only one industry. If the distribution is based on population Ecuador is assigned two industries, the propylene glycol and the caprolactam industries. The propylene glycol industry is assigned away from Chile. In being assigned the caprolactam industry, which is taken away from Peru, Ecuador gives up the dimethyl terephthalate industry, which is assigned to Colombia. The reallocation of the caprolactam and dimethyl terephthalate industries takes place because neither Peru nor Ecuador demonstrate strong comparative cost advantages in these industries as demonstrated by the small percentage differences between the upper bound on the weighted DRC and the weighted DRC for the respective allocations in Table 6.09.

Colombia is to be awarded either five or seven industries depending on whether the allocation is based on income or population. If assigned five industries, Colombia would demonstrate a comparative cost advantage in the carbon black, ethylene glycol, polyethylene, polyvinyl chloride, and acrylic fibers industries. An allocation constrained by population-based distributional constraints dictates that in addition to the five industries mentioned, the dimethyl terephthalate and polypropylene industries also be assigned to Colombia. These two industries would be assigned away from Ecuador and Chile.

Peru is assigned one more industry if the allocation is based on population than if it is based on income. Regardless of the basis for the allocation Peru is assigned the sodium cyanide, isopropanol, and ethanolamines industries. In addition to these three industries Peru is assigned the caprolactam industry if the allocation is based on income or it is assigned the tri- and perchloroethylene and the ABS and SAN resins industries. The tri- and perchloroethylene and the ABS and SAN resins industries are allocated to Venezuela if the allocation is based on income.

Chile and Venezuela are the two relatively more developed of the Andean Common Market countries. Being the richest, they would stand to gain the most from a distribution based on income. The industries awarded them under a system of distribution based on population would represent their minimum acceptable demands.

Venezuela is awarded the methyl methacrylate, 2-4 tolylene diisocyanate and the SBR and SBR latex industries if the allocation is based on population. Based on income, Venezuela is to receive seven industries and is assigned in addition to the three already mentioned the tri- and perchloroethylene, butanol, phenol, and ABS and SAN resins industries.

Chile is the poorer of the relatively more developed countries and does not demonstrate a comparative advantage in the same industries if the distributional constraints are based on population rather than on income. Based on population, Chile is assigned three industries: butanol, phthalic anhydride, and methanol. Assuming a redistribution to an allocation based on income it is noted that Chile retains only two of the three industries assigned it: phthalic anhydride and methanol. It gives up butanol to the richer Venezuela and receives propylene glycol and polyethylene from the relatively poorer Peru and Colombia.

Table 6.11 presents an industry allocation based on the assignment of the minimum acceptable number of industries to each country. This table is derived from Tables 6.9 and 6.10 and does not represent the solution to an allocation problem constrained by distributional requirements consisting of the minimum number of industries acceptable to each country.[4] The industry allocation of Table 6.11 only provides a suitable basis for further negotiations because not all industries are assigned.

The industry allocations presented in Tables 6.09 and 6.10 are not very sensitive to changes in the production costs in the various industries in the various countries. The sensitivity is relatively small if the large number of industries, twenty-two, to be assigned to six countries is taken into consideration.

Accompanying the general degree of insensitivity of the allocations to changes in production cost^c the assignments of some industries to some countries demonstrated very high degrees of insensitivity. Thus the DRCs[5] of the ethanol-amines industry in Peru and the 2,4 Tolylene diisocyanate industry in Venezuela would have to increase by more than 50 percent before the industries would be assigned to other countries in either of the allocation schemes presented in Tables 6.09 and 6.10. Similarly, whether constrained by either population or income restrictions, the assignment of the polyvinyl chloride, sodium cyanide, and the SBR and SBR latex industries to Colombia, Peru, and Venezuela respectively, is unaffected by DRC increases of less than 20 percent. Furthermore, of the 14 industries allocated to the same country given either population or income constraints four more, the ethylene glycol, the polyethylene, the acrylic fibers, and the isopropanol industries, do not change location as long as the DRCs do not change by more than 10 percent. Concentrating on the allocations of Tables 6.09 and 6.10 separately it is discovered that the production costs of polystyrene would have to increase substantially before the industry would be reallocated away from Bolivia in an allocation scheme constrained by income distributional constraints. Moreover, some of the industries that are not allocated to the same countries in both income- and population-constrained allocations present fair degrees of immobility as evidenced by the high degree of insensitivity of the assignment of the propylene glycol and of the tri- and per-

Table 6.11. The Industries Assigned to Each of the Member Countries in Accordance with the Minimum Number of Industries Acceptable by Each of the Countries

Country	Industry
Bolivia	Polystyrene
Ecuador	Dimethyl terephthalate*
Colombia	Carbon black Ethylene glycol Polyethylene Polyvinyl chloride Acrylic fibers
Peru	Sodium cyanide Isopropanol Ethanolamines Caprolactam*
Chile	Butanol* Phthalic anhydride Methanol
Venezuela	Methyl methacrylate 2-4 Tolylene diisocyanate SBR, SBR Latex
Not assigned	Propylene glycol Phenol ABS, SAN Resins Polypropylene Tri- and Perchloroethylene

*Not definite allocations. That is, industries not assigned to the same countries in Tables 6.09 and 6.10.

chloroethylene, butanol, phenol, and ABS and SAN resins industries to Chile and Venezuela in an income-constrained allocation. Finally, it is to be noted that there are 15 and 14 industry assignments in Tables 6.09 and 6.10, respectively, that are insensitive to cost changes of less than 10 percent.

V

The purpose of this section is to compare the costs of supplying the region with the products of the assigned industries given different allocation schemes. First, the allocation of industries given no distributional constraints will be presented and the costs of supplying the region from the industries thus allocated will be computed. Next, the cost of supplying the market with petrochemical products will be computed for each of the allocations of Tables 6.09 and 6.10. Finally, the costs of supplying the market from industries located in accordance with the industry allocation design formulated by the Junta del Acuerdo de Cartagena will be estimated.

Given no distributional constraints the industries of the petrochemical sector are assigned to the countries demonstrating the lowest DRCs for such industries. Such an allocation is presented in Table 6.12. Although such an allocation may not be acceptable in practice because industries may not be assigned equitably to all countries, the costs of supplying the area with the products of the assigned industries from such an allocation are the lowest from among all possible allocations.

An examination of Table 6.12 reveals that Colombia and Ecuador are assigned most of the industries and therefore indicates that Colombia and Ecuador have a comparative cost advantage in the production of petrochemicals. The column representing the country imposing the upper bound on the weighted DRC reveals that Bolivia also holds a comparative cost advantage relative to Peru, Chile, and Venezuela in the petrochemical sector. Due to the fact that within the petrochemical sector Colombia, Ecuador, and Bolivia have a comparative cost advantage, an allocation designed without distributional constraints would not prove acceptable to Peru, Chile, and Venezuela since these countries would not be assigned many industries.

Given the allocation of industries presented in Table 6.12, the total value added by the domestic resources in the production of the goods of the petrochemical sector can be computed. The total domestic value added in the industries of the petrochemical sector is given by the sum of the total domestic values added in each of the industries. This latter measure is obtained for each industry by multiplying the weighted DRC by the total international value added in that industry in the area. The total international value added in a specific industry is given by the product of the international value added per ton of product and the marginal quantities demanded in 1985.[6]

The total value added in 1985 in the industries allocated on the basis of absolute advantage is 471.2 million dollars. This figure is to be compared to the international value added in the allocated industries, 416.5 million dollars per year.

Although not strictly relevant the international value of the products of the allocated industries was determined. This figure is of interest as it provides further insight into the dimensions of the petrochemical program. The international value of the products of the allocated industries was estimated to be 700 million dollars.

Industry	Country	Weighted DRC (× 10^4)	Upper Bound for Weighted DRC (× 10^4)	Country Imposing Upper Bound	Percent Difference
Carbon black	Colombia	456.	464.	Ecuador	1.6
Sodium cyanide	Ecuador	35.	45.	Colombia	26.5
Tri- and Perchloroethylene	Colombia	30.	34.	Venezuela	9.6
Isopropanol	Ecuador	65.	69.	Bolivia	6.0
Butanol	Chile	96.	96.	Ecuador	0.0
Ethylene glycol	Colombia	197.	244.	Bolivia	23.9
Propylene glycol	Ecuador	181.	192.	Bolivia	6.1
Phenol	Ecuador	82.	86.	Bolivia	5.6
Methyl methacrylate	Ecuador	93.	95.	Colombia	2.4
Phthalic anhydride	Ecuador	92.	97.	Chile	5.4
Dimethyl terephthalate	Colombia	450.	450.	Ecuador	0.0
Ethanolamines	Colombia	9.	11.	Ecuador	16.7
2-4 Tolylene diisocyanate	Venezuela	46.	48.	Ecuador	4.8
Caprolactam	Ecuador	232.	306.	Peru	32.1
Polyethylene	Colombia	1753.	1960.	Bolivia	11.8
Polystyrene	Bolivia	268.	284.	Ecuador	5.8
ABS, SAN Resins	Colombia	17.	22.	Bolivia	39.9
Polyvinyl chloride	Colombia	2290.	2832.	Bolivia	23.6
Polypropylene	Colombia	120.	144.	Bolivia	20.0
SBR, SBR Latex	Venezuela	202.	223.	Colombia	10.5
Acrylic Fibers	Colombia	4169.	4690.	Bolivia	12.5
Methanol	Ecuador	431.	434.	Chile	0.7
Total		11,314.			

*To make the table comparable to other tables weighted DRCs rather than DRCs are presented. Neither the industry assignments nor their sensitivities to changes in costs are affected by this change because the weights for a particular industry are the same for all countries.

Reallocating the industries to different locations than those presented in Table 6.12 in order to meet distributional requirements involves increases in costs: the total domestic value added in the production of the same goods in the same quantities increases. The production of the same 416.5 million dollars per year worth of foreign exchange given an industry allocation constrained by distributional requirements based on income as presented in Table 6.09 costs 481.4 million dollars per year: 10.2 million dollars more than the costs of producing the same goods in industries allocated without distributional restrictions. Given an industry allocation designed subject to distributional constraints based on population, the cost of producing 416.5 million dollars per year worth of foreign exchange is 474.5 million dollars per year: only 3.3 million dollars more than producing the same goods given on industry allocation not restricted by distributional considerations. The cost of supplying the market given the allocation of Table 6.10 is slightly smaller than the cost of supplying the market given the allocation of Table 6.09 because in an allocation constrained by population-rather than income-based restrictions more industries are assigned to Colombia, Ecuador, and Bolivia which demonstrate a comparative cost advantage in the industries of the petrochemical sector.

The calculation of the costs of the allocation of industries designed by the Junta del Acuerdo de Cartagena is more complicated because in most instances the industries are assigned to two or more countries. Because of the division of industries the possible gains from economies of scale are lost: the investment costs are much larger for a number of smaller plants with a combined capacity equal to that of a larger one. These additional capital costs are however submerged in the measures of both domestic and international value added and therefore do not cause very great changes in the DRCs: the DRC measures the relative efficiency of domestic production to international production for given size plants. The additional capital costs for given domestic and international values added dictate that either the other noncapital factors of production earn less or that the industry in question be subsidized or not be established. The third alternative seems the more relevant as displayed by the nonexistence of many of the petrochemical industries in the individual countries because of the smallness of the markets.

In establishing the costs of supplying the area with products of the petrochemical industries given the allocation designed by the Junta, three assumptions are made. First, it is assumed that the industries assigned by the Junta would indeed be established and that these industries would produce at the same prices as industries assigned to only one country. Second, it is assumed that the market is divided equally between the countries assigned the same industry. Third, it is assumed that for any given industry in any given country the value added per ton is equal to the product of the international value added and the DRC computed on the basis of an industry being assigned to only one country. The effect of this third assumption is minimal since the DRCs are scarcely affected by capital costs.

The cost of producing the 416.5 million dollars worth of value added in 1985, given the allocation of industries designed by the Junta del Acuerdo de Cartagena, is 590 million dollars. This figure does not reflect the additional capital costs that would result from such an allocation. The investment requirements for the allocation of industries designed by JUNAC is 676.4 million dollars: 208.8 million dollars more than the investment requirement if the industries had not been broken up. If it is assumed that the opportunity cost of capital is 20 percent per year, the cost of producing 416.5 million dollars of value added per year is 632 million dollars per year. If the opportunity cost of capital is only 10 percent, the cost is 611 million dollars per year and if it is 30 percent, the cost is 653 million dollars per year.

The cost of supplying the area given the JUNAC allocation and an opportunity cost of capital of 20 percent, 632 million dollars per year, can be compared to the costs of supplying the area from allocations designed subject to numerical distributional requirements. The costs of supplying the area, given allocations designed to conform to distributional requirements based on income and population, are 481.4 and 474.5 million dollars per year respectively. Thus the cost of supplying the area given the JUNAC allocation is over 30% greater than the cost of supplying the area given the allocation designed subject to numerical distributional constraints. However, as will become evident in the next chapter and as will be discussed in Chapter VIII, numerical distributional constraints do not represent very tight distributional constraints and therefore do not cause but very small increases of costs over the lowest cost unconstrained solution.

VI

In this chapter it was proposed that the allocation model could be implemented with linear programming routines. However, it was also noted that the constraints of the allocation model have to conform to a number of restrictions if the model is to be solved with linear programming methods. In spite of the limitations imposed by the restrictions on the model, the advantages of the applicability of linear programming solution methods that provide information on the sensitivity of the solutions dictated the use of linear programming routines to:

1. Investigate the importance of transport costs.
2. Design industry allocations conforming to distributional requirements based on income or population.

The importance of transport costs was investigated in order to determine the relative importance of production costs and transportation costs in the determination of industry allocations. It was discovered that transport costs are relatively unimportant in determining the allocation of industries. Further, because production costs are the main determinants of industry allocations, these allocations are fairly insensitive to changes in transportation costs.

The model was implemented to formulate industry allocations that would minimize the costs of supplying the markets of the region and that would satisfy distributional constraints. Even though only allocations subject to numerical distributional constraints could be designed, these allocations can be employed as a possible basis for starting negotiations and as sources of information on the advantages of assigning specific industries to specific countries. The allocation of industries formulated on the basis of minimum industry requirements of each of the countries (Table 6.11) could be established as the basis for negotiations. This basic allocation could then be modified by the assignment of the nonassigned industries so as to achieve an allocation that would satisfy all members.

The industry allocations formulated also provide information on the comparative advantages of the various countries, on the sensitivity of the allocations to changes in costs, and on the costs of implementing different allocations. Fourteen out of twenty-two industries were assigned to the same countries in allocations constrained by requirements based on either income or population. The fact that these fourteen industries were assigned to the same countries indicates that some countries have fairly definite comparative advantages in some industries. The definiteness of these comparative advantages was further highlighted by the high degrees of insensitivity of some of the industry allocations to changes in the domestic resource costs. It was also determined that in general the allocations constrained by income-based restrictions were less sensitive to changes in costs than the allocations constrained by population-based restrictions. This smaller degree of sensitivity is the result of the fact that in income-based allocations 12 of the 22 industries are assigned to only two countries. This relative insensitivity to costs also dictates that the cost of supplying the region from industries allocated on the basis of income are slightly greater than the costs of supplying the region from industries allocated on the basis of population.

7 ALLOCATIONS OF INDUSTRIES GIVEN GENERALIZED DISTRIBUTIONAL CONSTRAINTS

The purpose of this chapter is to design industry allocations with the use of an integer program. The allocation model has to be implemented as an integer programming problem if the coefficients of the decision variables in the constraints are real numbers not restricted to the integer values of zero and one. The values of the coefficients of the decision variables cannot be restricted to zeroes and ones in distributional constraints based on the minimum requirements of the countries with respect to their shares of the total value added, the value of sales, or the investment requirement of the set of petrochemical industries in the area. The minimum requirements of the countries with respect to their shares of benefits are assumed equal to the lesser of the benefits accruing to them on the basis of either income or population. Given the minimum distributional requirements, allocations will be designed that conform to distributional requirements with respect to:

1. The total values added in the various industries in the various countries.
2. The total values of sales of the various industries in the various countries.
3. The investment requirements of the various industries in the various countries.

In the first section of this chapter a brief description of the solution routine employed for allocating industries will be presented. First, the general problem of determining optimal solutions to integer problems will be discussed. The solution method employed is identified and the reasons for its selection as the appropriate algorithm are presented.

In Section II the practical consideration of the termination of calculations is discussed. The integer programming computer program is stopped before all the calculations are completed because the completion of such calculations would require excessive computer time. Furthermore, because of the nature of the algorithm employed, a near optimal or possibly optimal solution is available when the computations are stopped and therefore the cost involved in the continuation of calculations may not be warranted.

In the third section the determination of minimum distributional constraints is discussed. The allocation was constrained by minimum distributional constraints in order to avoid the assignment of industries to countries demonstrating inefficiencies in these industries. The countries' demands for benefits in terms of value added, value of sales, or investment requirements should be small enough so that the assignment of industries to high-cost producers is unnecessary.

In the fourth section the allocation of industries designed subject to minimum distributional constraints with respect to value added is presented. The particular industry assignments are discussed and the total amounts of domestic value added assigned the countries are calculated. The sensitivity of the allocations to changes in costs is also determined. As is explained in Section IV, the sensitivity of the allocations is determined empirically by implementing the integer program each time one of the cost coefficients is changed. Finally, the total cost of the domestic resources employed to satisfy the region's demand for petrochemical products is calculated.

The optimal allocation of industries given minimum distributional constraints with respect to sales values is presented in Section V. In Section VI a similar allocation with constraints formulated in terms of investment requirements is described. In both sections the particular industry assignments of the allocations are discussed. However, no sensitivity analyses are performed for these assignments because the sensitivities of the assignments to changes in costs can only be determined empirically at considerable cost.

Section VII concludes this chapter with a brief comparison of the restrictiveness of the constraints and their effect on the costs of the different allocations designed.

I

The allocation model has to be implemented as an integer programming problem if the constraints are formulated in terms of total value added, the value of sales, or the investment requirements.[1]

The implementation of the model as an integer model is, however, much more difficult than the implementation of the model as a linear programming problem. Solution methods for integer programming problems have in general been based on either the branch-and-bound approach or the cutting plane approach. As indicated by Hillier and Lieberman, "many people feel that the most promising mode for integer programming algorithms is to use the *branch-and-bound technique* and related ideas to *implicitly enumerate* the feasible integer solutions."[2] In this section attention is focused on the branch-and-bound technique because it is the most promising of the two approaches and because the solution method employed in the implementation of the model is based on this technique.

Numerous solution procedures based on branch-and-bound techniques have been designed to determine the optimal solutions to integer problems. All of these procedures are based on the enumeration of solutions: solutions are examined and eliminated from further consideration until all possible solutions have been either implicitly or explicitly enumerated and the optimal solution has been determined. Although very clever enumeration procedures have been designed, "none possess computational efficiency that is even remotely comparable to the simplex method."[3]

The relative inefficiency of integer programming solution procedures has restricted the size of the problems that can be practically solved. Indeed, the size of integer problems is ordinarily limited to a few dozen variables because increases in the number of variables usually determine exponential increases in the numbers of possible solutions.

The solution procedure employed for the determination of the optimal solution to the allocation model was that formulated by Geoffrion as an improvement to the "additive algorithm" designed by Balas.[4,5] Specifically, the solution method employed is the same as the Balasian implicit enumeration method presented as the additive algorithm, except for the improvement formulated by Geoffrion. Thus, Geoffrion proposed the use of surrogate constraints obtained with linear programming methods to improve the efficiency of the Balasian algorithm.

The solution procedure developed by Balas and improved upon by Geoffrion was selected because it addresses itself directly to the problem of 0, 1 integer programming and is therefore expected to be the most efficient procedure for solving the allocation problem. Another advantage of the Balas-Geoffrion procedure is that it will usually provide near optimal solutions if the calculations are stopped before all the solutions are enumerated. In fact, the solution available at the time computations are terminated may be optimal: the remainder of the computation time required may just be necessary for the proving of the optimality of the solution by means of the exhaustive enumeration of all other possible solutions.

The accuracy of the statements with respect to the efficiency of the algorithm and regarding the fact that the algorithm provides near optimal solutions after a limited number of iterations can best be demonstrated by briefly describing the Balas-Geoffrion algorithm. First, the Balasian implicit enumeration algorithm is described.[6] Next, the improvement proposed by Geoffrion to improve the computational efficiency of the algorithm is described.

The Balasian algorithm is a solution procedure that is based on the branch-and-bound approach to integer programming. The solution approach of the Balasian procedure, like that of generalized branch-and-bound programs, is to define subsets of solutions from among the set of all possible solutions and, when possible, to eliminate some of these subsets from any further consideration. Indeed, assuming that the objective function is to be minimized to be specific, any set of solutions is subdivided into a number of subsets. These possible solutions based on these subsets are examined and a subset is eliminated if the possible solutions from the subset either violate the constraints or produce solutions that are larger than a previously determined minimum solution. If a subset cannot be eliminated because the solutions based on it do not violate any constraints or because the solutions based on it are not larger than the minimum previous solution, it means that a better solution has been found. This better solution is then stored as the incumbent against which other solutions are checked, and the subset from which this new solution was determined is also eliminated from further consideration. Then from among the subsets that were not eliminated a new set is chosen to be partitioned into subsets and the effort to try to eliminate subsets resumes.

In order to simplify the description of the Balasian algorithm as it deals with sets and subsets some terms are defined. A set S (of n variables) is partitioned into subsets that are called *partial solutions*. If a partial solution has m variables, $m < n$, then the other $(n - m)$ variables are called free variables. A completion of a partial solution is defined as a solution that is determined by the specification of the value of the free variables of the partial solution. Finally it is said that a partial solution is fathomed, eliminated from further consideration, if:

1. The partial solution has no completions that do not violate the constraints. That is, there are no feasible solutions.
2. No feasible completion of the partial solutions presents an objective function value that is less than the incumbent solution.
3. A feasible completion of the partial solution presents an objective function value that is better than that of the incumbent solution. In this case the completion replaces the incumbent solution.[7]

In order to utilize the Balasian algorithm for the minimization of the objective function to a 0, 1 integer program it is necessary that all the coefficients of the decision variables, $C_1, \ldots, C_n$, be positive and ordered so that $C_1 \leqslant C_2 \leqslant C_3, \ldots, \leqslant C_n$. If the coefficient of a given variable X_i is negative, the variable X_i is replaced by $(1 - X_i^1)$ so that the coefficient of X_i^1 is positive. The requirement that the variables be arranged so that $C_1 \leqslant C_2 \leqslant C_3, \ldots, \leqslant C_n$ does not restrict the applicability of the algorithm.

Given that the coefficients of the variables are positive and that the variables are ordered, the purpose of the algorithm in a minimization problem is to assign the value of zero to as many variables as possible. Thus, if there were no constraints the best solution would be that given by the set $(0, \ldots, 0)$. If lower bound constraints are given and it is necessary to assign the value of one to some variables, the algorithm will attempt to satisfy the constraints by assigning ones to the variables with the smaller costs.[8] The variables with the smaller costs are those with the smaller subscripts and thus the algorithm will begin trying to establish a feasible solution by assigning the value of 1 to the first variable and then to a second and so on.

Geoffrion proposed that the Balasian algorithm could be improved by the addition of surrogate constraints, computed from the original constraints, to aid in the implementation of the first fathoming rule. Thus Geoffrion proposed the formulation of surrogate constraints that would embody the information contained in the original constraints so as to make unnecessary the application of the first fathoming rule to each constraint individually.[9]

Given a minimization problem formulated as:
Minimize

$$Z = CX$$

subject to

$$b + Ax \geqslant 0$$

$$X_i = 0 \text{ or } 1 \tag{3}$$

where C and X are n vectors representing the cost coefficients and the decision variables respectively, b is an m vector representing the right-hand sides of the constraints, and A is a $m \times n$ matrix representing the coefficients of the decision variables in the m constraint equations, the surrogate constraints take the form:

$$u(b + Ax) + (\bar{Z} - CX) \geqslant 0 \tag{4}$$

where u is a non-negative m vector and $\bar{Z}$ is the value of the currently best known solution. The problem is the formulation of a series of surrogate constraints that are as strong as possible. A number of surrogate constraints have to be formulated during the solution of a problem because particular constraints are strong only relative to particular solutions: as the partial solutions to be tested change, new surrogate constraints have to be formulated.

A surrogate constraint $u^1(b + Ax) + (\bar{Z} - CX) \geqslant 0$ is said to be stronger than a constraint $u^2(b + Ax) + (\bar{Z} - CX) \geqslant 0$ if the maximum of the left-hand side of the first constraint is less than the maximum of the left-hand side of the second constraint. Therefore, the formulation of the strongest possible constraints requires the minimization of the maximum of $u(b + AX) + (\bar{Z} - CX) \geqslant 0$ over all $u \geqslant 0$.

The minimization is restricted by the fact that the values of the decision variables in the partial solution cannot be changed and that the free variables can only assume the values of zero and one. Therefore the problem can be written as: minimize

$$[\max \{u (b + AX) + (\bar{Z} - CX) \mid X_j = 0 \text{ or } 1 \text{ for } X_j \notin S$$

and

$$X_i = X_j^S \text{ for } X_j \in S\}] \tag{5}$$

where S represents the partial solution and X_i^S represents the elements in the partial solution. The problem of minimizing the maximum of the combination of the constraints can be transformed into a linear programming problem by rearranging equation 5 to read as:
Minimize

$$\sum_{i=1}^{m} u_i b_i^S + \bar{Z} - Z^S + \max \left\{ \sum_{J \notin S} \left(\sum_{i=1}^{m} u_i A_{ij} - C_j \right) X_j \mid X_j = 0 \text{ or } 1, j \notin S \right\} \tag{6}$$

Then, as pointed out by Geoffrion, the second part of equation 6 can be expressed by its dual as:

$$\min \left\{ \sum_{j \notin S} W_j \mid W_j \geqslant 0 \right.$$

and

$$W_j \geqslant \sum_{i=1}^{m} u_i A_{ij} - C_j, j \notin S \right\} \tag{7}$$

Then equation **6** can be rewritten as the linear program:
minimize

$$\sum_{i=1}^{m} u_i b_i^S + \bar{Z} - Z^S + \sum_{j \notin S} W_j$$

subject to

$$W_j \geqslant \sum_{i=1}^{m} u_i A_{ij} - C_j, j \notin S$$

and

$$W_j \geqslant 0, \ j \notin S$$

$$u_i \geqslant 0 \tag{8}$$

The solution of the linear program represented by the set of equations 8 will produce one of the following results:

1. The objective function is negative and therefore the surrogate constraint is infeasible.
2. The objective function is positive and the strongest surrogate constraint relative to S can be formulated from the u_is obtained.

Furthermore, in this case, if the dual variables are integer, the optimal solution to the integer program is given by these dual variables.

Within the framework of the Balasian algorithm outlined, the discovery that the surrogate constraint is infeasible would cause the fathoming of the partial solution being considered and the algorithm would backtrack to find new solutions. Similarly if the dual of the positive solution to the linear program is integer, a new solution is designed and fathomed and again the algorithm backtracks. If the partial solution is not fathomed, it is augmented and the process of trying to fathom the new solution is re-started with the surrogate constraint included as a constraint. Particular surrogate constraints are maintained for as long as desirable as determined empirically; thereafter these constraints are neglected.

Geoffrion empirically determined that the formulation and introduction of surrogate constraints greatly reduced the number of iterations necessary for the obtainment of feasible solutions with the Balasian algorithm. Thus in the solution of problems ranging in sizes from 20 variables and 4 constraints up to 80 variables and 11 constraints, the Balas-Geoffrion algorithm required between

5 to 10,000 times fewer iterations than the straight Balasian algorithm. The Balas-Geoffrion algorithm· also proves itself to be very efficient compared to other integer programming routines.

II

In practice in the implementation of the allocation model the Balas-Geoffrion algorithm was not allowed to complete all computations because of computer time limitations. The computations were stopped before all calculations were completed because the nature of the Balas-Geoffrion algorithm is such that usually near optimal solutions can be expected before all possible solutions have been enumerated. Indeed, empirically it was discovered that nearly optimal solutions could be obtained in as little as 30 seconds of execution time on an IBM 370–155 computer. This time, which seems to provide a reasonable trade-off between better solutions and increased computation costs, was subjectively determined through an analysis of the values of the best solutions available for an integer program when computations were terminated with different computation times and through the comparison of the best solutions of integer programs and the optimal solutions of the corresponding linear programs.

In order to examine the development of better solutions with longer computation times the allocation model with constraints formulated with respect to values added was executed for periods of 30 seconds, 1 minute, 3 minutes, and 10 minutes. In the first run the program was given a linear programming start. The linear programming start offers a quick first solution by rounding the values of the duals to the linear programming problem formulated by Geoffrion described in the last section. The inclusion of a reasonably tight upper bound facilitates the search for better solutions by excluding from analysis those solutions with lower bounds greater than the established upper bounds. The upper bound was set at 1.5 and represented a rather tight bound in that the solution to the corresponding linear program is 1.2449.[10] The 1, 3, and 10 minute programs were given the best solution calculated with the 30 second program as a starting point.

The integer program with a linear programming start and an upper bound discovered six solutions that were feasible and consecutively better in 317 iterations.[11] The first feasible and better solution, 1.3707, was obtained after 15 seconds of execution time. In the next 10 seconds the remaining 5 and always better solutions were found. The last solution before the program was stopped had a value of 1.3366.

The 1 minute program was given the best solution determined by the 30 second program as an initial solution. Thus, since the solution was feasible an upper bound of 1.3366 was automatically imposed. During 1 minute of execution time, the program carried out over 1000 iterations but did not find a better solution. The industry assignment designed by the 30 second program, which is equal to that obtained with the 1 minute program, is presented in Table 7.01.

The 3 minute program was initialized with the 30 second program solution and found one better solution with a value of 1.3321 in 120 seconds. In the remaining 60 seconds no better solutions were discovered. The industry assignment for the three minute program is also presented in Table 7.01.

The 10 minute program was also initialized with the 30 second program solution and discovered one more solution in addition to the solution already found with the 3 minute program. After obtaining the best solution to the 3 minute program, 1.3321, the program was executed for nearly 3 minutes before it ob-

Table 7.01. Allocations of Industries Obtained by Executing the Integer Program 30 Seconds, 3 Minutes, and 10 Minutes. The Minimization Was Restricted by Value Added Constraints

Industry	30 Seconds	3 Minutes	10 Minutes
Carbon black	Venezuela	Venezuela	Venezuela
Sodium cyanide	Ecuador	Ecuador	Ecuador
Tri-, and perchloroethylene	Venezuela	Venezuela	Venezuela
Isopropyl alcohol	Peru	Peru	Peru
Butanol	Venezuela	Venezuela	Venezuela
Ethylene glycol	Chile	Chile	Chile
Propylene glycol	Venezuela	Venezuela	Venezuela
Phenol	Venezuela	Venezuela	Venezuela
Methyl methacrylate	Venezuela	Venezuela	Venezuela
Phthalic anhydride	Chile	Chile	Chile
Dimethyl terephthalate	Ecuador	Ecuador	Ecuador
Ethanolamines	Colombia	Colombia	Ecuador
2,4 Tolylene diisocyanate	Venezuela	Ecuador	Ecuador
Caprolactam	Ecuador	Venezuela	Venezuela
Polyethylene	Chile	Chile	Chile
Polystyrene	Bolivia	Bolivia	Bolivia
ABS, SAN Resins	Venezuela	Ecuador	Colombia
Polyvinyl chloride	Peru	Peru	Peru
Polypropylene	Bolivia	Bolivia	Bolivia
SBR, SBR latex	Ecuador	Venezuela	Venezuela
Acrylic Fibers	Colombia	Colombia	Colombia
Methanol	Venezuela	Ecuador	Ecuador

tained a better solution with a value of 1.3316. In the remaining 5 minutes of execution time no better solutions were found.

The difference in the value of the solutions obtained after executing the program for 30 seconds or 10 minutes is only 0.0050, which represents a difference of only 0.0037 percent.[12] Thus it appears that the tests executed with the allocation model constrained by restrictions formulated with respect to value added corroborate the expectation that the Balas-Geoffrion algorithm provides near optimal solutions in short periods of time and before all computations are completed. Further, it also seems that execution periods of 30 seconds should be sufficient in such applications as sensitivity analysis or in the design of industry allocations of limited relevance.

The above stated conclusion regarding the efficiency with which the Balas-Geoffrion algorithm provides near optimal solutions is also limited but to a greater extent supported by the results of tests with models formulated with respect to sales values and investment requirements. Given a model restricted by sales value constraints, the value of the best solution obtained in a 30 second run is 1.3204, which is only 0.30 percent larger than the best solution to the 3 minute program, 1.3164. Given a model restricted by investment requirement constraints the value of the best solution obtained in 30 seconds is 1.2637 which is 0.97 percent larger than the best solution obtained by executing the program for 3 minutes, 1.2515.

The solutions to integer programs were compared to the solutions to the corresponding linear programs because the linear programming solutions determine the absolute smallest values the integer programming solutions can attain. In practice, however, the integer solutions are expected to be greater than the linear solutions because of the restriction that the solutions contain only integer numbers. Given distributional constraints formulated with respect to value added the minimum value of the objective function for a linear program is 1.2450 and the minimum value obtained with the integer program after 10 minutes of execution time is 1.3316. The difference between the two objective functions is 6.7 percent. For an allocation restricted by constraints based on sales values, the value of the optimal objective function of the linear program is 1.2343 and the value of the best solution to the integer program obtained in 3 minutes is 1.3164. The difference between the two objective functions is 6.4 percent. Finally, for an allocation restricted by investment requirement constraints the optimal value of the linear program is 1.1784 and the value of the best solution to the integer program obtained in 3 minutes is 1.2515. The difference between the two functions is 6.0 percent. The small values for the differences between the objective function values indicates that if not actually optimal, the solutions to the integer programs are at least very close to optimal.

III

The purpose of this section is to present the distribution of benefits dictated by the minimum requirements of the countries. The benefits to be distributed are taken to be represented by the value added, the sales value, or the investment requirements. Minimum country requirements are formulated in order to insure that the sum of the benefits required by the countries is smaller than the total of the benefits to be allocated.

The sum of the minimum country requirements has to be sufficiently smaller than the amount of the benefits to be distributed to insure that minimum cost allocations of industries will be designed. If the country requirements, represented by the distributional constraints, are too large the model will no longer be able to determine least cost solutions constrained by distributional requirements. Rather, the program will have to eliminate the lowest cost producers from consideration and assign the industries on the basis of comparative costs from among the group of high-cost producers.

The problem to be resolved is the formulation of distributional constraints small enough so that the model is not forced to higher cost solutions and yet large enough so as to make the distributional aims effective. It was estimated that an appropriate ratio between the sum of the countries' demands and the total benefits would be of the order of 80 percent. This figure was chosen because among the industries to be assigned the acrylic fibers, polyvinyl chloride and polyethylene industries are very large and exceed the country requirements: often the allocation of these industries reduces the size of the benefits to be allocated more than it reduces the country demands.

Minimum requirement constraints were formulated on the basis of the smaller of the country requirements based on income or population. The minimum acceptable share of benefits for the poorer countries is given by a distribution proportional to income and the minimum acceptable share for the richer countries is given by a distribution proportional to population. Table 7.02 presents the proportionate acceptable minimum benefits acceptable by the countries.

Although the sum of the percentage minimum country requirements only adds up to 77 percent of the benefits it was subjectively considered that such a ratio of demands for benefits to assignable benefits represents an adequate compromise between the requirement for tight distributional constraints to insure their effectiveness and the requirement for the slack needed to avoid the choice of high-cost solutions. In practice the allocation with respect to minimum country demands designs allocations that satisfy the distributional requirements and yet do not cause high-cost solutions. In the absence of distributional requirements the value of the objective function is 1.1335. The introduction of mini-

Table 7.02.   Minimum Acceptable Benefits

Country	Minimum Acceptable Percentage Share of Benefits
Bolivia	3.0
Chile	13.8
Colombia	20.0
Ecuador	5.0
Peru	18.2
Venezuela	16.2
	77.0

mum distributional requirements formulated with respect to value added causes the value of the objective function to increase to 1.3316 and signifies that the distributional constraints are reasonably tight. However, the constraints are loose enough so as to permit the allocation of 6 industries representing 47 percent of the total assignable value added to the countries demonstrating the lowest costs. Similarly, the introduction of distributional constraints formulated with respect to sales values causes the value of the objective function to increase to 1.3164 but yet allows the allocation of 7 industries according to absolute lowest costs. The introduction of distributional constraints based upon investment requirements causes the value of the objective function to increase to 1.2515 and allows for 8 industries to be allocated to the countries demonstrating lowest costs in those industries.

IV

In Chapter III it was proposed that distributional constraints could be formulated with respect to the values added of the different industries in the different countries. These constraints are of particular relevance because the countries probably define their benefits in terms of the increases in income attributable to the establishment of the various industries and their changes in income are expected to be proportional to the values added in the different industries. The allocation of industries given distributional constraints formulated with respect to value added was performed with the integer programming code described in the first section of this chapter. Given 10 minutes of execution time on the IBM 370–155 computer, the best solution obtained to the integer program dictates the allocation of industries presented in Table 7.03.

Table 7.03. Allocation of Industries on the Basis of Minimum Country Requirements with Respect to Value Added

Country		Percentage of DRC Increase That Would Not Affect Assignment
Bolivia	Polystyrene	20
	Polypropylene	20
Chile	Ethylene glycol	20
	Phthalic anhydride	20
	Polyethylene	less than 10
Colombia	ABS, SAN Resins	20
	Acrylic fibers	10
Ecuador	Sodium cyanide	20
	Dimethyl terephthalate	20
	Ethanolamines	20
	2, 4 Tolylene diisocyanate	20
	Methanol	20
Peru	Isopropyl alcohol	20
	Polyvinyl chloride	less than 10
Venezuela	Carbon black	20
	Tri-, perchloroethylene	20
	Butanol	20
	Propylene glycol	20
	Phenol	20
	Methyl methacrylate	20
	Caprolactam	20
	SBR, SBR latex	20

A salient feature of Table 7.03 is that Venezuela and Ecuador are assigned the majority of the industries as they are assigned 8 and 5 industries respectively. In turn Chile is assigned 3 industries and Bolivia, Colombia, and Peru are assigned 2 each. Although it is assigned the most industries, Venezuela is assigned the least in terms of the assignment of value added per year in excess to its minimum demand for value added per year.[13] Thus, as shown in Table 7.04 the ratio of assigned value added to minimum acceptable value added is least for Venezuela.

In terms of value added, Venezuela was not assigned very much, even though it was assigned 8 industries, because of the very limited size of some of the

Table 7.04.   Minimum Demands and Assignment in Terms of Value Added

Country	Minimum Country Demands in Terms of Value Added (Millions of Dollars/Year)	Value Added Assignment (Millions of Dollars/Year)	Ratio of Assignment and Minimum Demand
Bolivia	14.2	17.2	1.21
Chile	65.1	109.7	1.68
Colombia	98.2	174.3	1.77
Ecuador	23.6	40.6	1.72
Peru	85.9	136.5	1.59
Venezuela	76.4	76.4	1.00

industries assigned it.[14] The total domestic value added by Venezuela in each of two of the industries assigned it, tri- and perchloroethylene and propylene glycol, is only of the order of 1 million dollars per year. In each of the butanol, phenol, and methyl methacrylate industries the total domestic value added by Venezuela per year is of the order of only five million dollars. Venezuela, which demonstrates the third highest minimum country requirement as shown in Table 7.04, was not assigned any large industries and only 3 medium-sized industries:[15] the carbon black, the caprolactam, and the SBR and SBR latex industries with total domestic values added per year of 24.6, 17.9, and 8.4 million dollars respectively.

Ecuador is assigned a fairly large number of industries, five, in accordance with the fact that Ecuador often demonstrates a comparative cost advantage in the industries to be assigned as presented in Table 6.12 of the last chapter. In contrast to Venezuela, however, Ecuador demonstrates the second highest ratio of value added assigned to value added demanded as shown in Table 7.04. Although 4 of the 5 industries assigned Ecuador—sodium cyanide, dimethyl terephthalate, ethanolamines and 2, 4 tolylene diisocyanate—are small with values added of less than 5 million dollars per year, and the fifth industry, methanol, is only medium-sized with a value added of 17.9 million dollars per year, the ratio of assigned value added to minimum acceptable value added for Ecuador is relatively large because Ecuador's minimum demand for value added is relatively small.

Chile was assigned three industries, the ethylene glycol, the phthalic anhydride, and the polyethylene industries. These three industries represent a total domestic value added in Chile of 109.7 million dollars per year and dictate that the ratio of value added assigned to value added demanded for Chile be the third largest. The value contributed by these industries is relatively large because of the inclusion of the polyethylene industry, which is very large and alone accounts for a domestic value added per year of 93.7 million. Further, the ethylene glycol industry is not small but rather medium sized with a value added of 10.2 million dollars per year. The phthalic anhydride industry is small, however, and contributes only 4.9 million dollars of domestic value added per year.

Colombia and Peru are assigned only 2 industries each. However, one of the two industries assigned each of these two countries is one of the very large industries. Colombia is assigned the acrylic fibers industry, which presents a domestic value added of 174 million dollars per year; Peru is assigned the polyvinyl chloride industry, which demonstrates a domestic value added of 133 million dollars per year. The other two industries assigned Colombia and Peru, the ABS and SAN resins and the isopropyl alcohol industries, are small and contribute values added of only 0.7 and 2.9 million dollars per year respectively. Because of the assignment of the acrylic fibers industry to Colombia, the ratio of the value added assigned to the value added demanded is the largest for Colombia. Because the value added in the polyvinyl chloride industry relative to Peru's demand for value added is smaller than the value added in the acrylic fibers industry relative to Colombia's demand for value added, the ratio of the value added assigned to the value added demanded for Peru is smaller than that for Colombia. However, even though the ratio for Peru, 1.59, is only the fourth largest, it is only 10.7 percent smaller than the ratio for Colombia and therefore indicates that Peru's demands in terms of value added are amply satisfied.

Bolivia, like Colombia and Peru, is also assigned only 2 industries. The industries assigned Bolivia, polystyrene and polypropylene, are only medium sized, however, and Bolivia's value added in the assigned industries is only 11.2 and 6.0 million dollars per year respectively. However, Bolivia's minimum demand in terms of value added is small and therefore the assignment of the polystyrene and polypropylene industries more than satisfied this demand and the ratio of value added assigned to value added demanded for Bolivia is 1.21.

In order to determine the effects of changes in the coefficients of the objective function of the model on the industry allocation presented in Table 7.03, the sensitivity of the individual industry assignments to increases in costs in the corresponding countries was investigated by implementing the program each time one of the coefficients was changed. The determination of the sensitivity of the allocations is so cumbersome because the solution procedure to the integer program, unlike the simplex solution method for linear programs, does not simultaneously provide a dual solution with the primal solution. For each of the 22 industries the sensitivity of the assignment of an industry to a particular country was determined empirically by increasing the DRC of the industry in the assigned country by 20 percent and executing the program for 30 seconds. In each of the trials the program was given an initial solution corresponding to the industry allocation presented in Table 7.03. As discussed in Section II of this chapter, given a good initial solution, 30 seconds of execution time appears to be more than sufficient for the determination of the sensitivity of industry assignments. However, given only 30 seconds of execution time, it must be noted that the results regarding the sensitivity of an assignment have to be regarded only as very likely because such results have not, however, been determined with absolute certainty.

Except for 3 industries the industry assignments presented in Table 7.03 are insensitive to cost changes of up to 20 percent. The industry allocation of Table 7.03 is sensitive to cost increases of 20 percent in the polyethylene industry in Chile, in the polyvinyl chloride industry in Peru, and in the acrylic fibers industry in Colombia. In fact, the industry allocation of Table 7.03 is sensitive to cost increases of 10 percent in the polyethylene industry in Chile and in the polyvinyl chloride industry in Peru: it is insensitive to a 10 percent cost increase in the acrylic fibers industry in Colombia. If costs in the acrylic fiber industry in Colombia increase by 20 percent, the acrylic fibers industry is reassigned to Peru. Colombia, in turn, is compensated with the polyvinyl chloride industry that is taken away from Peru. However, since the value added in the polyvinyl chloride industry in Colombia is not sufficient to satisfy Colombia's minimum demand for value added, Colombia is also assigned the polypropylene industry that is taken away from Bolivia. Bolivia, in turn, to satisfy its demand for value added exchanges the polystyrene industry with Venezuela for Venezuela's SBR and SBR latex industry.

The assignments of the polyethylene and polyvinyl chloride industries to Chile and Peru are more sensitive and a 10 percent increase in costs causes the industries to be reassigned. A 10 percent increase in costs in the polyethylene industry in Chile causes the polyethylene industry to be reassigned to Peru. Chile is compensated with the polyvinyl chloride industry, which is taken away from Peru. Similarly, a 10 percent increase in costs in the polyvinyl chloride industry in Peru would lead to the same industry exchange.

In the previous chapter it was established that the international value added by the domestic production of the products of the petrochemical sector in 1985 is 416.5 million dollars per year. It was also determined that given an opportunity cost of capital of 20 percent per year, the cost of supplying the area with the same products in the same quantities given the allocation of industries designed by the Junta del Acuerdo de Cartagena is 632 million dollars per year. These figures can be compared to the cost of supplying the area given the allocation of industries presented in Table 7.03, 554.6 million dollars per year. More detailed cost comparisons are made in Chapter VIII where the costs for all proposed allocations are compared.

V

The purpose of this section is to present the minimum cost allocation of industries conforming to restrictions formulated with respect to sales. The industries of the petrochemical sector are assigned so as to fulfill minimum country demands with respect to sales.

The assignment of industries on the basis of minimum country demands corresponds to the first of the two possible sets of constraints that can be formulated on the basis of sales.

$$\sum_i D_i \, Z_i^k \geqslant \frac{Y^k}{Y_M} \sum_k \sum_i D_i Z_i^k$$

for countries $m = 1, \ldots, K^*$, the countries with relatively low incomes per capita, and

$$\sum_i D_i \, Z_i^k \geqslant \frac{\text{pop}^k}{\text{pop}^M} \sum_i \sum_k D_i Z_i^k$$

for countries $m = K^* + 1, \ldots, K$, the countries with relatively high incomes per capita.

D_i = value of total marginal demand for product i in the free trade area.

Z_i^k = dichotomous variable that takes on the value of 1 when industry i is assigned to country k and 0 otherwise.

Y^k = income in country k.

Y^M = income of the free trade area.

pop k = population of country k.

pop M = population of the free trade area.

A second possible set of constraints that could be formulated with respect to sales are sales equalization constraints:

$$\sum_{j \neq k} \sum_i D_i^j \, Z_i^k - \sum_{j \neq k} \sum_i D_i^k Z_i^j = |E|$$

D_i^j = demand for product i by country j.

Z_i^k = dichotomous variable that takes on the value of 1 when industry i is assigned to country k and zero otherwise.

E = constraint reflecting an allowable margin of error.

The model was implemented to design industry allocations conforming to the first rather than the second set of constraints for three reasons. First, the first set of constraints appears more relevant since they are formulated according to prescribed distributive norms. Second, the implementation of the model subject to the second set of constraints is likely to determine industry allocations that would be unacceptable to Bolivia and Ecuador because their demands are very small relative to those of the other four countries and therefore Bolivia and Ecuador might not be assigned any industries. Further, it is expected that an allocation designed subject to the second set of constraints will tend to perpetuate rather than ameliorate the relative differences in the sectorial development between the different countries. Third, it is anticipated that an allocation of industries designed subject to the first set of constraints will be more similar to the industry allocation designed subject to value added constraints. Such a similarity is useful because a comparison of the allocations reveals the consistency of the allocations.

The constraints formulated on the basis of minimum country demands with respect to sales do not reflect the total impact of the implementation of the petrochemical program on the countries' balances of payments because they do not take into account the value of the imported intermediate imports utilized in the manufacture of the products of the program. If in addition to the sales values the costs of the intermediate imports necessary to produce the products of the petrochemical program were considered, measures like the value added measures of the last section would be obtained. Therefore, in this section the effect of the imported intermediate inputs on the balance of payments is ignored. Although sales values do not present the total impact on the balances of payments of the countries of different industry assignments, sales values are easily measurable and therefore are appropriate for the formulation of distributional constraints.

The optimal allocation of industries conforming to distributional constraints formulated in terms of sales values is presented in Table 7.05.

The allocation of industries presented in Table 7.05 is very similar to that of Table 7.03. In Table 7.05, 15 out of the 22 industries are assigned to the same countries as in Table 7.03. The allocations that are different in Tables 7.03 and 7.05 are:

1. The sodium cyanide and ethanolamines industries are assigned to Peru in Table 7.05 rather than to Ecuador as in Table 7.03. Further, the 2,4 tolylene diisocyanate industry is assigned to Venezuela in Table 7.05 rather than to Ecuador.
2. The ethylene glycol and propylene glycol industries are assigned to Colombia and Chile in Table 7.05 rather than to Chile and Venezuela.

Table 7.05. Allocation of Industries on the Basis of Minimum Country Requirements with Respect to Sales Values

Country	*Industry*
Bolivia	Polystyrene
	ABS, SAN Resins
Chile	Propylene glycol
	Phthalic anhydride
	Polyethylene
Colombia	Ethylene glycol
	Polypropylene
	Acrylic fibers
Ecuador	Dimethyl terephthalate
	Methanol
Peru	Sodium cyanide
	Isopropyl alcohol
	Ethanolamines
	Polyvinyl chloride
Venezuela	Carbon black
	Tri-, perchloroethylene
	Butanol
	Phenol
	Methyl methacrylate
	2, 4 Tolylene diisocyanate
	Caprolactam
	SBR, SBR Latex

3. Colombia and Bolivia exchange the ABS and SAN resins and the polypropylene industries: the ABS and SAN resins industry and the polypropylene industry are assigned to Bolivia and Colombia respectively in Table 7.05.

The difference in allocations between Tables 7.03 and 7.05 does not appear to follow any definite pattern. Although in 4 cases industries were assigned to lower cost countries in Table 7.05 than in Table 7.03, three industries were assigned to higher cost countries. Moreover, the sales values are roughly proportional to the values added and therefore the reason for the difference in the allocations is not apparent.

As presented in Table 7.06, the ratio of sales value assigned to sales value

Table 7.06.   Minimum Demands and Assignments in Terms of Sales Value

Country	Minimum Country Demands in Terms of Sales (Millions of Dollars/Year)	Sales Assigned (Millions of Dollars/Year)	Ratio of Assignment to Minimum Demand	Value Added Assigned (Millions of Dollars/Year)
Bolivia	22.8	24.3	1.07	12.1
Chile	105.0	169.6	1.62	106.6
Colombia	159.0	248.4	1.56	187.2
Ecuador	38.1	63.8	1.67	36.6
Peru	139.0	241.2	1.74	138.6
Venezuela	124.0	135.0	1.09	67.8

demanded is greatest for Peru and therefore Peru is proportionately assigned the most in terms of sales. Ecuador demonstrates the second highest ratio and is followed by Chile and Colombia. The demands in terms of sales of Venezuela and Bolivia are minimally met as demonstrated by the low ratios of sales assigned to sales demanded.

In terms of value added assigned, Colombia and Peru are assigned more given the industry allocation of Table 7.05 as compared to the industry allocation of Table 7.03. The other four countries, Bolivia, Chile, Ecuador, and Venezuela, are assigned less in terms of value added in Table 7.05 than in Table 7.03.

The cost of the domestic resources employed in satisfying the area with the products of the petrochemical industries assigned is 548.2 million dollars per year, given the industry assignments of Table 7.05. This cost is slightly lower than that given the industry allocation of Table 7.03, 554.6 million dollars per year.

VI

In this section the allocation of industries obtained by restricting the model with distributional constraints formulated in terms of investment requirements is presented. Although, in general, countries are not expected to want to maximize their investment expenditures, they might want to do so if the expenditures can be financed with low interest loans or if they are interested in increasing investment due to macroeconomic considerations.

Given distributional constraints formulated with respect to investment, the optimal allocation of industries is presented in Table 7.07.

As compared to Table 7.03, the following changes were introduced in Table 7.07:

1. The ABS and SAN resins and the polyvinyl chloride industries were reassigned away from Colombia and Peru and the butanol and propylene glycol industries were reassigned away from Venezuela to be allocated to Chile.
2. The 2,4 tolylene diisocyanate, methanol, and ethanolamines industries

Table 7.07. Allocation of Industries on the Basis of Minimum Country Requirements with Respect to Investment

Country	Industry
Bolivia	Polystyrene
Chile	Butanol
	Propylene glycol
	Phthalic anhydride
	ABS, SAN Resins
	Polyvinyl chloride
Colombia	Ethylene glycol
	Polyethylene
	Acrylic fibers
Ecuador	Sodium cyanide
	Dimethyl terephthalate
Peru	Isopropyl alcohol
	Ethanolamines
	Caprolactam
	Polypropylene
Venezuela	Carbon black
	Tri-, perchloroethylene
	Phenol
	Methyl methacrylate
	2,4 Tolylene diisocyanate
	SBR, SBR Latex
	Methanol

were reassigned away from Ecuador. The first two were reassigned to Venezuela and the third to Peru.

3. The ethylene glycol and the polyethylene industries were reassigned from Chile to Colombia.

4. Lastly, the caprolactam and polypropylene industries were reassigned away from Venezuela and Bolivia to Peru.

Since the required investment in each industry is taken to be the same in all countries, the industry reassignments introduced by Table 7.07 are such as to lower the costs of supplying the area and seven of the eleven industries reassigned were reallocated to lower cost countries. Moreover, two of the four industries that were reassigned to higher cost countries, the ABS and SAN resins and the ethanolamines industries, are very small and the other two, the polypropylene and methanol industries, are among the smaller of the medium-sized industries. The largest reduction in costs, 28.6 million dollars per year, was achieved by the reassignment of the polyethylene and polyvinyl chloride industries to Colombia and Chile. Since the butanol, ethylene glycol, propylene glycol, 2,4 tolylene diisocyanate, and caprolactam industries are all among the smaller medium-sized industries, the reduction in costs achieved by the reassignment of each of these industries is not very large and is only of the order of one or two million dollars per year.

The fact that the investment requirement of the industries to be allocated is not correlated to the value added in each of the industries in each of the countries, in this case permits the design of an allocation that exhibits lower costs. Furthermore, it must be noted that the fact that the investment requirements increase only to the .6 power of the volume of production tends to permit lower cost allocations.[16] Thus, the cost of the domestic resources employed to satisfy the demands for the products of the assigned industries given the allocation of Table 7.07 is 521.2 million dollars per year. This figure can be compared to the cost figure given the allocation of Table 7.03, 554.6 million dollars per year.

With respect to the countries' investment requirements Ecuador is assigned the most followed by Bolivia and Colombia as presented in Table 7.08. The ratios of the assigned investment requirements to the investment demands for Venezuela, Chile, and Peru are fairly close to one signifying that their demands were only minimally satisfied. In terms of value added, compared to the allocation of Table 7.03, Colombia and Chile gain by an assignment such as that of Table 7.07. In turn the other four countries lose but Peru loses in particular because it loses the polyvinyl chloride industry to Chile and is in turn assigned high investment requirement but low value added industries.

Table 7.08. Minimum Demands and Assignment in Terms of Investment Requirements

Country	Minimum Country Demands in Terms of Investment Requirements (Millions of Dollars)	Investment Requirements Assigned (Millions of Dollars)	Ratio of Assigned Requirements and Minimum Demanded Requirements	Value Added Assignment (Millions of Dollars/Year)
Bolivia	14.2	25.4	1.79	11.2
Chile	65.1	69.2	1.06	142.9
Colombia	98.2	152.2	1.55	254.3
Ecuador	23.6	47.0	1.99	20.1
Peru	85.9	89.5	1.04	24.9
Venezuela	76.4	84.3	1.10	68.7

VII

In this chapter it was noted that the cost of supplying the area with the products of the assigned industries is highest for the allocation designed subject to value added constraints, 554.6 million dollars per year. The cost of supplying the area with the same products given an allocation designed subject to sales value constraints is somewhat less, 548.9 million dollars per year, and the cost given an allocation designed subject to investment requirement constraints is even less, 521.2 million dollars per year.

The cost of an allocation designed subject to constraints formulated with respect to either values added, sales values, or investment requirements depends on the restrictiveness of such constraints. The value added constraints are the most restrictive because the coefficients of the decision variables in the constraints are but for a scaling factor identical to the coefficients of the decision variables in the objective function. The constraints designed with respect to sales values are the second most restrictive because in general the values of sales will be roughly proportional to the values added: in as far as there are discrepancies opportunities for reassignments and savings appear. The investment requirement constraints are the least restrictive because the investment requirements are fairly independent of the values added.

8 SUMMARY AND CONCLUSIONS

In the first chapter of this study it was proposed that one of the fundamental questions to be resolved in integration schemes among less developed countries is that of the distribution of benefits. Further, it was noted that the countries subscribing to an integration scheme consider the main benefits of such schemes to be derived from the localization of new industries within their borders. The benefits to be derived from an expanded trade in the products already traded are expected to be very limited.

The concern of the participating countries with the location of new industries has been recognized most explicitly in the Andean Common Market. The Cartagena Agreement, the treaty establishing the Andean Common Market, proposed the formulation of Sectorial Programs of Industrial Development in order to allocate the industries of selected sectors among the member countries. However, the negotiation of these programs has proved very difficult and therefore programs for only two out of the seven sectors selected for such programs have been ratified.[1]

Even if the negotiators could settle upon acceptable distributional criteria, a major problem confronting the negotiators of such programs would still be the lack of adequate data on which to base allocations. At the same time, the implementation of a number of models designed for the rational allocation of these industries is also hindered by the same data considerations.

The investment criterion developed by Bruno and Krueger, the Domestic Resource Cost criterion, was selected as the most appropriate for the development of a model designed to allocate the industries of the Sectorial Programs of Industrial Development of the Andean Common Market. The criterion developed by Bruno and Krueger was nominally modified by dividing the calculated DRC by the exchange rate. Since this modification only affects the basis of comparison—instead of comparing the DRC to the shadow exchange rate, the modified DRC is compared to 1—the modified DRC, utilized from now on, is simply referred to as the DRC.

The fact that makes the DRC criterion practicable for the allocation of a large number of industries in several countries is that the DRC criterion is virtually identical to the Corden measure of effective protection. The implementation of a model based on the DRC criterion as formulated by Bruno and Krueger would have been hindered by the same data problems that have made the implementation of most other programs designed to allocate the industries of the Andean Common Market impracticable: it is difficult to determine the costs of the factors of production as well as the costs of the nontraded inputs. The Corden measure of effective protection, which is equal to the DRC minus one, is given by the ratio of the domestic value added and the international value added minus one. Taking domestic prices to be equal to international prices plus tariffs, the domestic value added per unit of output evaluated at domestic prices is given by the differences between the value of output and the value of the tradable inputs. The international value added is given by the difference between the value of output and the value of inputs evaluated at international prices. Both the domestic value added and the international value added measures are corrected for imported capital charges and for the returns accruing to foreign investors.

The model developed for the allocation of industries is an integer programming model. The objective function of the model seeks to minimize the weighted sum of the DRCs for all industries in all countries; the weights are given by the ratio of the international value added in the industry and the total international value added in all the assigned industries. The minimization is constrained by three types of constraints: first, constraints insuring that all industries are allocated; second, constraints determining monopolistic allocations of industries; and third, distributional constraints designed to insure that the countries are assigned industries according to predetermined distributional objectives. Since it is not clear what benefits the countries participating in integration schemes expect from the assignment of industries, several types of distributional constraints were formulated. First, constraints were designed to allocate industries as identical entities to the countries: the number of industries assigned each country was determined by the country's income relative to the income of the area in one case, and by the country's population relative to the population of the area in a second case. Second, distributional constraints were formulated with respect to values added, sales values, and investment requirements and the countries were assigned amounts of value added, sales values, and investment requirements according to minimum country requirements equal to the minimum accruing the countries on the basis of either income or population.

II

The model was utilized to design industry allocations that minimize the cost of supplying the area with the products of the industries of the petrochemical programs subject to distributional constraints. The advantages of designing the industry allocations with the model are that relatively low-cost allocations are designed and that these allocations are designed systematically with clearly defined distributional objectives. The costs of supplying the area given the industry allocations designed with the model were always less than the costs of supplying the area given the industry allocations designed by the Junta del Acuerdo de Cartagena (JUNAC). As compared to the strict distributional objectives to which the allocations designed with the model were restricted, the distributional objectives of the Junta del Acuerdo de Cartagena as revealed by their allocation of industries appear to be very confused.

In order to simplify the allocations of industries and the calculation of the costs of the various allocations, it was assumed that the industries would be designed to satisfy the projected 1985 demands of the area and that these demands would be completely inelastic. The projected international value of the demand for products of the assigned industries in 1985 is 700 million dollars. Given the establishment of the assigned industries in the area, the international value added by the domestic factors of production in the fulfillment of the 1985 demands of the various products is 416.5 million dollars.

The total value added by the domestic factors or the cost of the domestic factors employed in a particular industry in a particular country is given by the product of the DRC for that industry in that country, the international value added per unit in that industry in that country, and the number of units demanded in the area. The total domestic value added in all industries in all countries is given by the sum of the total domestic values added of the assigned industries in the assigned countries.

The costs associated with different industry allocations were determined from the costs of the domestic factors employed in the production of the products of the assigned industries in the assigned countries.

The cost of satisfying the area given the allocation of industries designed by the Junta del Acuerdo de Cartagena is equal to the cost calculated in the manner delineated above plus the cost of the additional capital required due to the splitting-up of industries. In order to calculate the total domestic value added in the manner described above three assumptions were made. First, it was assumed that the industries would indeed be established. Second, it was taken that the market would be divided equally between the countries assigned the same industry. Third, it is assumed that for any given industry in any given country the value added per ton is equal to the product of the international value added and the DRC computed on the basis of an industry being assigned to only one country. Because particular industries were not always assigned to only one country, the allocation of industries designed by JUNAC requires a higher initial capital investment and therefore the opportunity cost of this additional capital has to be added to the cost of the other domestic resources employed in the production of the products of the assigned industries.

In Table 8.01 the costs of the allocations performed subject to the various distributional constraints are presented. In Table 8.02 the costs associated with the JUNAC allocation are presented given that the opportunity costs of capital are assumed to be 10, 20, or 30 percent.

An examination of Tables 8.01 and 8.02 reveals that the costs of the industry allocations designed with the model are in all cases less than the cost of the

Table 8.01. The Costs Associated with the Various Allocations Designed with the Model

Type of Distributional Constraint Restricting the Allocation	Table in Which Allocation is Presented	Cost (Millions of Dollars Per Year)
No distributional constraint	6.12	471.2
Population-based numerical constraint	6.04	474.5
Income-based numerical constraint	6.06	481.4
Constraint with respect to investment requirements	7.07	521.2
Constraint with respect to sales values	7.05	548.2
Constraint with respect to value added	7.03	554.6

Table 8.02. The Costs Associated with the Allocation of Industries Designed by the Junta Del Acuerdo de Cartagena (Table 4.02)

Domestic Value Added (Millions of Dollars per Year)	Additional Required Invest-ment (Millions of Dollars)	Opportunity Cost of Capital (Percent)	Total Cost (Millions of Dollars Per Year)
590	210	10	611
590	210	20	632
590	210	30	653

industry allocation designed by JUNAC given opportunity costs of capital of either 10, 20, or 30 percent per year. Furthermore, the costs of supplying the area are also always less than the cost of supplying the area given the JUNAC allocation even if the additional capital costs resulting from the higher initial investment are ignored. Thus, the savings in terms of costs given the model allocation rather than the JUNAC allocation result not only from capital cost savings but also from savings resulting from the allocation of industries to the countries with comparative cost advantages.

The allocations of industries designed with the model were restricted by the distributional objectives presented in Table 8.03. An analysis of Tables 8.01 and 8.03 suggests that the costs of supplying the market are smaller when the degree of correlation between the coefficients of the decision variables in the constraints and those in the objective function is small. This results because, in the cases considered, constraints not related to the objective function are less restrictive and it is possible to satisfy the distributional requirements by the assignment of low cost industries. Thus, the allocations constrained by numerical distribution constraints based on either population or income demonstrated the lowest costs among all the allocations because it was possible to satisfy the industry demands of the high cost countries with the relatively small industries, while the relatively large industries were assigned to the relatively lower cost countries.

Investment requirements demonstrate some correlation with the total values added in the industries. Therefore, an allocation restricted by distributional constraints formulated with respect to investment determines an 8 percent higher cost for supplying the area than that given by an allocation designed subject to numerical constraints. Since sales values demonstrate an even greater degree of correlation with the total values added the cost of supplying the area subject to distributional constraints formulated with respect to sales values is

Table 8.03. Distributional Objectives Restricting the Allocations Designed with the Model

Country	Population Numerical — Least Number of Industries Assigned Country	Income Numerical — Least Number of Industries Assigned Country	Investment Requirements — Minimum Investment Assigned Country (Millions of Dollars)	Sales Value Requirements — Minimum Sales Value Assigned Country (Millions of Dollars/Year)	Value Added Requirements — Minimum Value Added Assigned Country (Millions of Dollars/Year)
Bolivia	2	1	14.2	22.8	14.2
Chile	3	4	65.1	105.0	65.1
Colombia	7	5	98.2	159.0	98.2
Ecuador	2	1	23.6	38.1	23.6
Peru	5	4	85.9	139.0	85.9
Venezuela	3	7	76.4	124.0	76.4

5 percent higher than the cost of supplying the area given an allocation designed subject to investment constraints.

The highest cost allocation designed with the model is that obtained by subjecting the model to value added requirements. This results because the value added in an industry represents the cost of the domestic resources employed in that industry and therefore the total value added requirements of the countries represent requirements that certain amounts of the costs incurred in the production of the products of the petrochemical program be attributable to domestic factors of those countries.

The industry assignment program designed by the Junta del Acuerdo de Cartagena determines the distributions of values added, sales values, and investment requirements presented in Table 8.04. The distributions of benefits patterns of Table 8.04 do not indicate that there was any logical basis for the distribution. With respect to value added Peru is assigned inordinately much in comparison to Chile, which was assigned even less than Ecuador. Colombia is also assigned a large percentage share of the benefits but this corresponds to Colombia's large share of either the population or income of the area. The value added assignments for Colombia, Venezuela, Ecuador, and Bolivia do however conform fairly well with a distribution based on population.[2]

Given the JUNAC distribution, Bolivia, Chile, and Ecuador are assigned relatively more and Colombia, Peru, and Venezuela are assigned relatively less with respect to sales values than with respect to value added. Like the distribution with respect to value added, the distribution with respect to sales values assigns very little to Chile, which is assigned even less than Ecuador. If the ordering of Chile and Ecuador is interchanged, the distribution with respect to sales values demonstrates an ordinal ordering conforming to a distribution based on population. Although the rearranged ordering conforms to an ordering based on population, it is noteworthy that both Chile and Venezuela, the relatively richer countries, appear to receive proportionately less than their share of benefits on the basis of population.

In terms of investment requirements Ecuador is again assigned more than Chile and in this sense the distribution does not conform to a distribution based on population. In fact Ecuador is assigned as much as Venezuela. Although Colombia and Peru are assigned investment requirements roughly proportional to their populations, Venezuela and Chile are assigned proportionately less and Ecuador and Bolivia proportionately more than would be dictated by a distribution based on population. Thus it appears that the poorer countries, Bolivia and Ecuador, gain at the expense of Chile and Venezuela and that the poorer countries are assigned even more than would be dictated on the basis of population alone at the expense of the richer countries.

However, it must be noted that the similarities between the JUNAC distribu-

Table 8.04. Benefit Distributions Corresponding to the Allocation of Industries Designed by the Junta del Acuerdo de Cartagena

Country	Value Added (Millions of Dollars/Year)	Percent Share of Value Added	Sales Value (Millions of Dollars/Year)	Percent Share of Sales Value	Investment Requirement (Millions of Dollars)	Percent Share of Investment
Bolivia	45.76	7.8	78.94	8.7	68.7	10.2
Chile	53.52	9.1	98.06	10.9	72.2	10.7
Colombia	159.55	27.1	247.22	27.7	199.4	29.6
Ecuador	54.83	9.3	101.34	11.4	101.4	15.0
Peru	175.81	29.9	240.96	26.9	131.3	19.5
Venezuela	98.85	16.8	129.34	14.4	100.8	15.0

tion and the distributions based on population are probably coincidental. Further, although a number of objectives could be conjectured from the distributions determined by the JUNAC allocation and from segments of the allocation, the JUNAC allocation does not reveal any clearly defined distributional objectives.

III

Finally, some directions for future research suggested by an examination of the model and of the results of this study need to be delineated. First, the method for allocating industries developed in this study could be strengthened by:

1. The empirical demonstration of the equivalence of domestic prices and international prices plus tariffs.
2. The correction of the DRC estimates of the various countries for the distortions caused by nontariff restrictions.

The first of these two questions (which are obviously interrelated) determines whether the method suggested for estimating the cost of the domestic factors employed in an industry in a particular country is appropriate. The domestic value added by the domestic resources per unit of output is given by the difference between the domestic price of output and the sum of the contributions of the products of the input coefficients for the tradable inputs and the domestic prices of these inputs. The domestic prices were taken to be equal to international prices plus tariffs as suggested by the theory of international trade. However, it would obviously be useful if this relationship between international prices and domestic prices was empirically proven.

In this work it was assumed that tariffs represented the only restrictions on imports and that there are no other restrictions. The allocations of industries designed with the model would not be affected if this assumption was relaxed to allow for equal amounts of non-tariff protection in the various countries. Corrections should be made if the levels of non-tariff protection in the different countries are different even if it is assumed that the amounts of non-tariff protection are equal across all goods in any one country.

These non-tariff restrictions, which can be viewed as distortions of the shadow rate of foreign exchange for any one country, affect all the DRCs. Thus the DRCs are higher or lower as determined by an undervalued or overvalued exchange rate caused by non-tariff subsidies or restrictions. In allocations of industries among countries the countries relying most on non-tariff restrictions would be favored as they would appear to have comparative cost advantages. In order to eliminate this distortion it would be useful to determine the levels of non-tariff protection in the various countries and to correct the DRCs accordingly.

The distortions caused by varying degrees of non-tariff protection are greatest when there are no distributional constraints or when these are not related to the values added. If the constraints restricting the allocation are formulated with respect to value added and are relatively tight and do not allow very much slack between the total of the value added requirements and the total assignable value added the distortion caused by non-tariff restrictions is minimal. The distortion in the allocation of industries given value added constraints is minimal because the value added constraints incorporate the same distortions as the objective function.

A second area of research suggested by this study deals with the possible extensions of the model. First, it would be useful to apply the model to allocate other industries with different technical characteristics in order to further test the validity of the approach employed. The model could be applied, for example, to the Metalworking Program of Sectorial Development of the Andean Common Market. Second, the model could be employed to simultaneously allocate industries in a number of different sectors. Very useful policy information could be derived by using the model to simultaneously allocate all the industries of the Sectorial Programs of Industrial Development. Third, the model could be employed to allocate industries in any other integration schemes that adopt industry assignment schemes for distributional purposes.

APPENDICES

A TECHNOLOGICAL ASPECTS OF THE ALLOCATED INDUSTRIES

The purpose of this section is to describe the technological production aspects of the industrial entities assigned in the simplified industrial allocation program by the Junta del Acuerdo de Cartagena. Since often there exists more than one production process, the justification for the choice of one process as the representative is indicated. Emphasis in these descriptions is placed on the identification of those processes that simultaneously produce two or more of the products originally assigned by JUNAC and that were aggregated into more meaningful production units.

The production processes determine the necessary inputs. The input coefficients per ton of output are then presented. Also the representative capacities of plants are presented.

The inputs to the production of some goods as well as the uses of these goods determine which industries should be vertically integrated. The description and breakdown of the usage of goods are therefore presented.

The descriptions and the data presented relating to production processes, input coefficients, and usage patterns were derived mainly from the following sources: Lowenheim and Moran's *Faith, Keyes, and Clark's Industrial Chemicals;*[1] Albert V. Hahn's *The Petrochemical Industry: Market and Economics;*[2] and the *Kirk-Othmer Encyclopedia of Chemical Technology.*[3] No effort is made to identify the sources of all the descriptions and all the data when these are of a general character; however, specific entries are duly indicated.

Although the data on production processes, inputs, and output usage derived from the above mentioned sources pertain mainly to the petrochemical industry in the U.S., they are applicable to the examination of the prospective establishment of these industries in the Andean Common Market. The reason for the applicability of the data is that all the ACM countries would have to rely on imported technology and imported capital equipment to establish petrochemical industries. The new technology and capital equipment in the U.S. is very similar to that of other sources capable of supplying technology, like Europe or Japan: in the petrochemical industry new processes replace the old regardless of national boundaries. Thus, although the processes for obtaining the necessary petrochemical feedstocks differ in the U.S. and Europe and Japan, the processes for the production of more complex chemicals based on these feedstocks are very much alike.

The first of the products allocated in the petrochemical program is carbon black. Carbon black, which is very similar to ordinary soot, is basically elemental carbon made to conform to specifications with respect to particle size, surface characteristics, and degree of particle agglomeration. It can be produced by any of four processes that determine its characteristics. However, one process, the furnace process, accounts for over 90 percent of the total production of carbon black both in the U.S. and worldwide.[4] The channel process is an older process that has been mostly abandoned while the thermal process and the pyrolysis of acetylene processes are utilized only for the production of carbon blacks with exceptional characteristics.

The production of one ton of carbon black only requires—in addition to the usual capital, labor, energy, and other services—about 2100 liters of oil. Oil is considered a domestic input and therefore in the calculation of DRCs its value is not subtracted from the domestic or international value added in the production of carbon black. Plants designed for the production of carbon black range in capacity from 15,000 metric tons per year to the newer, larger plants with capacities of up to 390,000 metric tons per year.[5]

The main use of carbon black is in the production of elastomers, substances having the properties of rubber. Thus of the total of carbon black produced in the U.S. in 1974, 94 percent was used in the production of elastomers; 2.5 percent in the production of inks; 0.5 percent in the production of paints; and 3 percent in other uses.[6]

Carbon black was not vertically integrated with styrene-butadiene rubber (SBR) and SBR latex because even though SBR and SBR latex are elastomers they do not constitute the most significant part of the field. Furthermore, the very significant demand for carbon black in the Andean Common Market previous to any production of SBR and SBR latex in the region suggests that it has other more important markets in the region.

The reaction of hydrogen cyanide with sodium hydroxide produces sodium cyanide and water. The production of one ton of sodium cyanide theoretically requires 551.5 kilograms of hydrogen cyanide and 816.1 kilograms of sodium hydroxide. These figures were determined from examination of the chemical reaction. In practice in industry there are losses as reactions are not always carried to absolute completion. Therefore, based on industrial figures for similar reactions, the quantities of hydrogen cyanide and sodium hydroxide per ton of sodium cyanide were increased to 575 kilograms and 1100 kilograms respectively.

Sodium cyanide is commercialized in the form of white deliquescent crystals. The main uses of sodium cyanide are in electroplating, as an oxidizing reagent for gold extraction and in organic syntheses, the artificial production of naturally occurring substances.

Trichloroethylene and perchloroethylene are general solvents and cleaning agents that can be produced in several ways. Thus trichloroethylene can be produced together with perchloroethylene through the oxychlorination of ethylene dichloride and chlorine. Alternatively it can be produced from the reaction of acetylene and chlorine although this process is no longer competitive because of the increased price of acetylene. Therefore, over 90 percent of the production of trichloroethylene is based on the oxychlorination of ethylene dichloride and chlorine.[7] Perchloroethylene can be produced together with trichloroethylene as described above or it can be obtained by either the chlorination of hydrocarbons like propane or ethane or from acetylene and chlorine via trichloroethylene. Like the production of trichloroethylene from acetylene, the production of perchloroethylene from acetylene is no longer competitive. The bulk of perchloroethylene is therefore produced by oxychlorination of ethylene dichloride and chlorine and by the chlorination of hydrocarbons; the relative importance of these two processes could, however, not be determined.

The oxychlorination of ethylene dichloride and chlorine was taken to be the necessary process for the production of tri- and perchloroethylene because the process is definitely the main process for the production of trichloroethylene, as well as an important process for the production of perchloroethylene. The choice of this production process dictated that the trichloroethylene and the perchloroethylene industries should be aggregated as one industry. The inputs required for one ton of perchloroethylene and 793 kilograms of trichloroethylene are 1195 kilograms of ethylene dichloride, 642 kilograms of chlorine and 388 kilograms of oxygen.[8] In this case, for the calculation of DRCs, oxygen was taken to be a definitely domestic input whose production would be determined by requirements for it.

Trichloroethylene and perchloroethylene are both cleansing agents that have gained wide acceptance because of their quick drying and low flammability. Perchloroethylene is the more stable of the two and finds its main use in dry cleaning where it has displaced carbon tetrachloride. Trichloroethylene is more unstable and more likely to ruin clothing by decomposing to hydrochloric acid. The main use of trichloroethylene is in the vapor degreasing of fabricated metal parts. In 1974 in the U.S. 75 percent[9] of the production of perchloroethylene and 87 percent[10] of the production of trichloroethylene were used in dry cleaning and vapor degreasing respectively.

Isopropyl alcohol is made from propylene in much the same way as ethanol is made from ethylene. Sulfuric acid is used as a catalyst to absorb propylene and form propyl sulfate, which is then hydrolized with water to produce isopropyl alcohol and dilute sulfuric acid. In the industrial production of isopropyl alcohol losses occur and the inputs per ton of isopropyl alcohol are therefore estimated at 900 kilograms of propylene and 12.5 kilograms of sulfuric acid.[11]

The main use of propyl alcohol was as a basis for the subsequent production of acetone. However, the production of acetone as a by-product of the production of phenol by the oxidation of cumene has to a large extent displaced acetone produced via isopropyl alcohol. Moreover, the production of acetone directly from propylene with the Wacker process further threatens the production of acetone from isopropanol.[12] The demand for isopropyl alcohol is therefore declining. The other uses of isopropyl alcohol are as a solvent for oils, gums, shellac, and synthetic resins. These latter uses accounted for only 55 percent of the total of isopropyl alcohol used in the U.S. in 1974 with the balance being used for the production of acetone.[13]

Butanol was formerly produced by fermentation with the Fernbach process.[14] Production with this process only accounts for a small portion of total production at this time. A newer process, yet not the main one, consists of the hydration of crotonaldehyde, which is produced synthetically from the condensation of acetaldehyde. The main process, accounting for two thirds of production in 1974[15] and chosen here as the representative production process, consists of the catalytic hydration of n-butyraldehyde. The latter is obtained by the oxonation of propylene and synthesis gas. Thus, the production of one ton of butyl alcohol requires 762 kilograms of propylene and 782 cubic meters of synthetic gas.[16] In the calculation of the DRCs synthesis gas is treated as a home good.

Butanol has many and varied uses. In the U.S. in 1974 the use pattern[17] was:

Solvent	25%
n-Butyl acetate	10%
Glycol ethers and esters	15%
Plasticizers	10%
Amine resins	15%

Butyl acrylate and	
butyl methacrylate	15%
Miscellaneous and export	10%
	100%

Ethylene glycol, diethylene glycol, triethylene glycol, and polyethylene glycol were assigned separately by the Junta del Acuerdo de Cartagena in their allocation scheme for the petrochemical industry. Ethylene glycol and the higher homologs are all produced simultaneously in one plant by the high pressure hydration of ethylene oxide. The ratio of ethylene glycol to the higher homologs is determined by the ethylene oxide to water molar ratio: the greater the proportion of ethylene oxide, the greater the proportion of the higher homologs.

The ethylene oxide and ethylene glycols industries are treated as one vertically integrated industry for two reasons. First, most ethylene glycol producers start from ethylene and produce their own ethylene oxide. Second, of the total ethylene oxide produced, over 60 percent is used for the production of ethylene glycols. The production of one ton of ethylene glycols requires 900 kilograms of ethylene and a lot of air.[18]

The bulk of the production of ethylene glycol goes into the production of antifreeze (50 percent) and into the production of polyester fibers (35 percent).[19] Diethylene glycol is mainly used in the production of polyurethane and unsaturated polyester resins. Other uses of diethylene glycol are in the production of textile agents and in petroleum solvent extraction. Triethylene glycol is employed in natural gas dehydration, as a humectant, and in the production of solvents and vinyl plasticizers. Polyethylene glycol is used as a rubber and polyvinyl chloride lubricant and demolding agent and in hair creams and hydraulic fluids.

The propylene glycol, dipropylene glycol, and polypropylene glycol industries can be aggregated into one industry, the propylene glycols industry. Propylene glycols are produced by the hydration of propylene oxide in a process that is essentially the same as that used for the production of ethylene glycols. Propylene oxide is vertically integrated into the propylene glycols industry in much the same way that ethylene oxide was integrated into the ethylene glycols industry. Thus, it is taken that the production of one ton of propylene glycols requires 717 kilograms of propylene.

Propylene glycol finds its main application in the production of polyester resins. It has displaced ethylene glycol as a cellophane plasticizer and a tobacco humectant because of regulations regarding the use of the latter due to its toxicity. The most important use of dipropylene glycol is as another cellophane plasticizer. Polypropylene glycol is used in brake fluids because of its excellent viscosity and temperature characteristics.

The characteristic of the petrochemical industry of rapid technical change is reflected in the many available processes for the manufacture of phenol. Phenol was originally obtained by coal tar distillation. This process whereby natural phenol is produced accounts for less than 2 percent of the total production of phenol today.[20] The first process for producing synthetic phenol consisted of the sulfonating of benzene to produce benzenesulfonic acid, which was then neutralized and alkalisulfonated, and reacted with caustic soda to produce phenol. This process was replaced by two processes that consisted of the hydrolization of chlorobenzene with first sodium carbonate and later caustic soda. These processes were then replaced by the Raschig process, but it became obsolete in 1971 when the cumene peroxidation and toluene oxidation processes were adopted. The cumene peroxidation process is the most important at this time and accounts for 88 percent of the phenol production.[21]

The cumene peroxidation process was taken to be the most probable process to be utilized if a phenol plant were to be established in the Andean Common Market. Therefore the DRC calculations were based on this process. Simultaneously with phenol, acetone is produced with this process and is valued as an output rather than a worthless by-product since there always exists a market for acetone. It was taken that the production of cumene is vertically integrated with the production of phenol so that the production of one ton of phenol together with 610 kilograms of acetone requires 1104 kilograms of benzene and 593 kilograms of propylene.[22]

The largest use of phenol is in the production of phenolic resins, which are plastic-like mixtures of phenol and formaldehyde. These resins have very important uses as molding materials in objects that need to be functional rather than attractive since it is impossible to color these resins. The fact that they cannot be colored accounts for the fact that they have been replaced by more expensive materials that can be colored in such uses as telephone sets. These resins are also used in the production of marine and exterior plywoods. Also many adhesives are manufactured from these resins. Other important uses of phenol are in the production of caprolactam and bisphenol-A, a substance used in the production of phenolic and epoxy resins.

Although methyl methacrylate can be produced by isobutylene oxidation, the bulk of it is produced from acetone and hydrogen cyanide. The main requirements for the production of one ton of methyl methacrylate are: 581 kilograms of acetone, 270 kilograms of hydrogen cyanide, 320 kilograms of methanol, and 981 kilograms of sulfuric acid.[23]

The most important outlet for methyl methacrylate is in the production of cast sheet that is employed for outdoor signs, windows, and skylights. Methyl methacrylate is also used for the production of surface coatings like water-thinned paints and for moldings such as automobile tail lights and mercury lamp street-lights.

There are two very similar processes for the production of phthalic anhydride based on the oxidation of either naphathalene or ortho-xylene. The main process, naphathalene oxidation, has been gradually replaced by ortho-xylene oxidation because of the increased availability of ortho-xylene derived from petroleum and the scarcity of the relatively cheaper coal-tar based naphathalenes. Petroleum based naphathalenes are more expensive than ortho-xylene. The production of one ton of phthalic anhydride requires 975 kilograms of ortho-xylene and 2500 cubic meters of air.[24]

The main use of phthalic anhydride is as a plasticizer and it is the most important plasticizer. Plasticizers are compounds added to polymerise materials to impart upon them certain characteristics. Other uses of phthalic anhydride are in the production of alkyl resins used for coatings and polyester resins.

Dimethyl terephthalate (DMT) and terephthalic acid (TPA) are both obtained from the oxidation of p-xylene. In the production of DMT, TPA can be regarded as an intermediate input that can be isolated or converted to DMT. The uses of DMT and TPA are also similar. DMT and TPA are almost exclusively used in the production of polyethylene terephthalate fibers and film. The similarity of production processes and uses therefore warranted the aggregation of these two industries.

The process chosen for the production of DMT and TPA was that pertaining to the production of DMT because of the much greater demand for DMT. The requirements for the production of one ton of DMT are 670 kilograms of p-xylene and 400 kilograms of methanol.[25]

Although allocated separately by the Junta del Acuerdo de Cartagena, monoethanolamine, diethanolamine, and triethanolamine are all products of one plant and thus the industry, ethanolamines, should be treated as one. Ethanolamines are produced by reacting between one and three moles of ethylene oxide with ammonia to produce the three ethanolamines. The ratio of the three ethanolamines is determined by the relative amounts of ethylene oxide and ammonia and the reaction conditions. It was taken that 800 kilograms of ethylene oxide and 280 kilograms of ammonia were the appropriate ratio for the production of one ton of ethanolamines.

Monoethanolamine finds its main application as a scrubbing agent for removing acid constituents from gas streams. Diethanolamine is used in liquid detergents as the foam-creating element of these detergents. The main use of triethanolamine is in cosmetic formulations.

There is only one main process for the production of 2,4-tolylene diisocyanate and it consists of reacting 2,4-tolyldiamine with phosgene. It is taken that the producers of 2,4-tolylene diisocyanate have captive sources of 2,4-tolyldiamine and phosgene. Therefore, one ton of 2,4-tolylene diisocyanate requires 687 kilograms of toluene, 942 kilograms of chlorine, and 209 kilograms of nitric acid.[26]

The main application of 2,4-tolylene diisocyanate is like that of all other diisocyanates as an input to the production of polyurethanes. Polyurethanes are commercialized as foams used as cushioning material in automobiles and furniture and for insulation in construction.

Caprolactam is the monomer of nylon 6. It is produced from the reaction of cyclohexanone, ammonia, carbon dioxide, sulphur, and oleum in air with the presence of a catalyst. The specific amounts of inputs per ton of caprolactam are: 890 kilograms of cyclohexanone, 1460 kilograms of ammonia, 520 kilograms of carbon dioxide, 680 kilograms of sulphur, and 1350 kilograms of oleum.[27]

The sole use of caprolactam is in the production of nylon 6, also called polycaprolactam. Nylon 6 is one of the two major types of nylon and its main applications are in the production of carpets and textiles.

Polyethylene was the first polyolefin plastic to be commercialized and is still the most important in terms of the amount of it consumed worldwide. It is the most important worldwide but is not necessarily so in all countries, as the relative amounts of polyethylene and polyvinyl chloride consumed are determined largely by the relative degree of development of the countries. In the developed countries polyethylene is the more important of the two, while the situation is the reverse in less developed countries. Polyethylene is more important in developed countries because of the trends in the packaging of goods and commodities in these countries. In the less developed countries, polyvinyl chloride is the more important because of its uses in more essential products like flooring, piping, and roofing.

There are two types of polyethylene, high density and low density, and they are produced by different processes. High density polyethylene is produced with a low pressure process while low density polyethylene is produced by a high pressure process. Low density polyethylene is characterized by a low softening point, high impact strength, and great flexibility. These characteristics make it ideal for such applications where constant rigid dimensions are not desired as in squeeze bottles and snap-cap closures. High density polyethylenes have higher softening points and are more rigid than low density polyethylenes. These characteristics dictate that it be used for products where less flexibility is desired as in containers such as trash cans or liquid detergent bottles.

Although high and low density polyethylene are produced by different methods and have different characteristics they were aggregated into one industry because the inputs are similar and because it was assumed that whichever country had a comparative advantage in one would also have a comparative advantage in the other. Another argument for treating low density and high density polyethylene as one industry is that the exact line of demarcation between high density and low density polyethylene, a specific gravity of 0.94, is quite arbitrary. Although the production processes might differ for very high or very low density polyethylenes, for polyethylene with specific gravities close to 0.94 the same process is used. Therefore, the amount of ethylene used for the production of one ton of the polymer was taken to be the average of the inputs to the production of the high and low density polyethylenes: 1150 kilograms of ethylene per ton of polyethylene.

Polystyrene, as its name indicates, is the polymer of styrene. The production of polystyrene is the main use of styrene and therefore in the analysis of industry allocation styrene and polystyrene are treated as one vertically integrated industry. Benzene is alkylated with ethylene to produce ethylbenzene, which is then catalytically dehydrogenated to produce styrene; the styrene is then polymerized to produce polystyrene. Assuming only minor losses in the polymerization of styrene, the required inputs per ton of polystyrene are 865 kilograms of benzene and 320 kilograms of ethylene.[28]

Polystyrene's great advantage over other plastics is its low price; it is also the cheapest thermoplastic. Therefore polystyrene finds its main application as foams utilized for insulation and packaging. Thus in the U.S. in 1965, of the total production of polystyrene 24 percent was used for insulating board, 12 percent for insulating cups, 18 percent for molding, 20 percent for building, and 7 percent for other miscellaneous uses.[29]

Although the major part of the production of styrene is utilized for the production of polystyrene, there are other important uses of styrene such as in the production of acrylonitrile-butadiene-styrene (ABS) and styrene-acrylonitrile (SAN) resins. In the U.S. in 1974, 10 percent of the production of styrene was utilized for the production of ABS and SAN resins.[30]

ABS resins are the most important of the new family of plastics called engineering plastics, which are plastics that have higher softening points, greater tensile strength, and better aging properties. These properties permit the use of ABS resins in fields in which polyethylene and polyvinyl chloride cannot be employed.

The most important uses of ABS resins are in automotive parts such as instrument panels and substitutes for chromed metal parts. The second most important use of ABS resins is as general purpose plumbing pipes and fittings. ABS resins are also employed in the manufacture of food-cabinet and door liners of refrigerators and in the production of housings for such appliances as openers and blenders.

SAN resins are also members of the new family of engineering plastics. The market for SAN resins, however, is much smaller than that for ABS resins:

whereas the production of ABS resins in the U.S. in 1965 was of 80,000 tons, the production of SAN resins was only of 14,000 tons.[31] The main use of SAN resins is in the production of dinnerware.

ABS and SAN resins are treated together in the analysis of the allocation of industries in the Andean Common Market because they were treated together by the Junta del Acuerdo de Cartagena. The two industries were probably aggregated by JUNAC because of the small demand in the area for these resins. The sum of the demands for these resins in the area in 1974 was of 741 tons.[32]

The aggregation of the ABS and SAN resins into one industry poses a problem for the determination of the input coefficients per ton of product because the products are different and have different inputs. It was taken that the input coefficients for the ABS resin industry were those of the whole industry because of the much greater importance of ABS resins. Therefore, assuming minimal polymerization losses, it was taken that per ton of product 500 kilograms of styrene, 250 kilograms of acrylonitrile, and 250 kilograms of butadiene are required.

The polyvinyl chloride (PVC) industry is vertically integrated with the vinyl chloride and ethylene dichloride industries because the bulk of ethylene dichloride is used in the production of vinyl chloride monomer, which in turn is used for the production of PVC. The inputs required per ton of PVC are therefore: 520 kilograms of ethylene and 1320 kilograms of chlorine.[33]

PVC resins have a great demand and are employed in building and construction, household uses, consumer goods, electrical uses, packaging, and transportation. Thus PVC is used to make: weather stripping and water pipes and fittings; furniture upholstery and garden hoses; inflatables, balls, and phonograph records; wire and cable coatings; food wraps; and automobile seat covers and floor mats.

Polypropylene can basically be produced by only one process developed by Montecatini, who licensed most of the world's producers.[34] Propylene is polymerized at low pressures in a hydrocarbon solvent using aluminum alkyl and titanium chloride as catalysts. Disregarding catalyst losses, the only input to the production of polypropylene is propylene.

Except for its lower specific gravity, polypropylene is very much like polyethylene and therefore its uses are very much the same. Polypropylene is mainly used for injection molding and for the production of fibers.

Styrene-butadiene rubber (SBR) is the most important synthetic rubber and accounts for over 70 percent of the total production of synthetic rubber.[35] It is a copolymer of styrene and butadiene where the two inputs are 30:70 by weight. Therefore the production of one ton of SBR takes 300 kilograms of styrene and 700 kilograms of butadiene.

The main use of SBR is in the production of tires and tire related items. Other minor uses are in mechanical goods, shoes, and foam.

In the analysis of the allocation of industry in the Andean Common Market the acrylic fibers and polyacrylonitrile industries were aggregated into one because polyacrylonitrile is only used to make fibers that are classified as acrylic fibers. These industries were also vertically integrated with the acrylonitrile industry because the bulk of the production of acrylonitrile is employed in the production of acrylic fibers. The production of one ton of acrylic fibers requires 1175 kilograms of propylene and 475 kilograms of ammonia.[36]

Acrylic fibers compete for markets with wool and silk. The main uses of acrylic fibers are in the production of rugs and carpets, blankets, and other woven and knit products.

Methanol is produced from the reaction of carbon monoxide and hydrogen under high pressures. The input requirements for one ton of methanol are: 1170 cubic meters of hydrogen.[37]

The use pattern of methanol in the U.S. in 1974 was the following.[38]

Formaldehyde	45%
Dimethyl terephthalate	10%
Methyl methacrylate	8%
Methylamines	4%
Methyl halides	4%
Acetic acid	4%
Solvents	10%
Miscellaneous and export	15%
	100%

B THE INTERNATIONAL PRICES OF THE VARIOUS PRODUCTS

Product	Price (Dollar/Ton)
Carbon black	234
Sodium cyanide	742
Tri- and perchloroethylene	364
Isopropyl alcohol	229
Butanol	375
Ethylene glycol	502
Propylene glycol	507
Phenol	595
Methyl Methacrylate	695
Phthalic Anhydride	520
Dimethyl Terephthalate	585
Ethanolamines	716
2-4 Tolylene Diisocyanate	937
Caprolactam	1,224
Polyethylene	573
Polystyrene	645

Product	Price (Dollar/Ton)
ABS, SAN Resins	937
Polyvinyl chloride	761
Polypropylene	662
SBR, SBR Latex	762
Acrylic Fibers	2,724
Methanol	117
Sodium Hydroxide	276
Hydrogen Cyanide	380
Styrene	423
Benzene	249
Ethylene	213
Aluminum Chloride	430
Chlorine	141
Ethylene Dichloride	242
Vinyl Chloride	198
Hydrogen Chloride	419
Propylene	162
Sulfuric Acid	408
Butyraldehyde	529
Acetone	309
p-Xylene	342
o-Xylene	180
Ethylene Oxide	573
Ammonia	195
Toluene	192
Nitric Acid	196
Cyclohexanone	271
Sulfur	93
Oleum	47
Acrylonitrile	518
Butadiene	391

Note: Refer to page 71 for an explanation of the sources and applicability of these prices.

C THE TARIFFS ON VARIOUS PRODUCTS IN THE ACM COUNTRIES IN AD VALOREM TERMS

	Percent					
Product	Bolivia	Chile	Colombia	Ecuador	Peru	Venezuela
Carbon black	35	20	15	10	36	40
Sodium cyanide	24	25	20	0	43	5
Tri- and Perchloro-ethylene	32	45	15	5	56	5
Isopropanol	24	25	30	10	48	150
Butanol	24	10	15	0	56	5
Ethylene glycol	24	35	5	15	50	50
Propylene glycol	24	25	30	15	50	50
Phenol	22	25	25	5	46	20
Methyl methacrylate	24	25	15	10	53	20
Phthalic Anhydride	26	10	25	0	49	80
Dimethyl terephthalate	26	45	5	0	64	80
Ethanolamines	26	30	15	15	49	14
2-4 Tolylene Diiso-cyanate	26	45	15	0	45	10
Caprolactam	26	30	32	0	45	35
Polyethylene	27	35	10	18	53	60
Polystyrene	27	55	47	18	52	60
ABS, SAN Resins	27	30	10	18	53	60
Polyvinyl chloride	27	30	10	18	50	60
Polypropylene	27	25	10	18	52	60
SBR, SBR Latex	36	30	5	18	61	.5
Acrylic Fibers	24	35	10	35	47	150
Methanol	24	20	15	10	86	25
Sodium hydroxide	22	20	30	10	56	107

Note: Refer to pages 71–72 for an explanation of the determination of these tariffs.

Product	Percent					
	Bolivia	Chile	Colombia	Ecuador	Peru	Venezuela
Hydrogen cyanide	24	35	20	0	45	5
Styrene	32	25	5	0	49	1
Benzene	32	20	30	0	52	1
Ethylene	32	20	5	0	49	.1
Aluminum Chloride	24	35	20	10	54	2
Chlorine	24	20	23	0	60	50
Ethylene dichloride	32	35	10	5	106	1
Vinyl Chloride	32	45	10	5	68	1
Hydrogen Chloride	24	35	26	10	54	2
Propylene	32	20	5	0	49	.1
Sulfuric Acid	66	20	1	25	150	15
Acetone	24	35	15	10	50	5
p-Xylene	32	20	10	0	50	10
o-Xylene	32	20	10	0	56	10
Ethylene Oxide	32	35	25	0	46	20
Ammonia	30	20	10	0	108	107
Toluene	32	20	10	0	55	10
Nitric Acid	24	20	26	0	174	50
Cyclohexanone	32	20	5	0	48	.1
Sulfur	50	10	10	50	100	50
Oleum	66	20	1	25	591	15
Acrylonitrile	24	45	15	0	57	35
Butadiene	32	20	5	0	46	.1

D TOTAL INTERNATIONAL VALUE ADDED IN THE INDUSTRIES OF THE PETROCHEMICAL PROGRAM

Industry	International Value Added (Millions of Dollars)
Carbon black	15.2
Sodium cyanide	1.5
Tri- and perchloroethylene	1.3
Isopropyl alcohol	1.2
Butanol	3.5
Ethylene glycol	7.3
Propylene glycol	5.7
Phenol	2.8
Methyl methacrylate	3.1
Phthalic anhydride	3.4
Dimethyl terephthalate	17.2
Ethanolamines	0.3
2-4 Tolylene diisocyanate	1.8
Caprolactam	11.5
Polyethylene	66.4
Polystyrene	8.2
ABS, SAN Resins	.5
Polyvinyl chloride	86.5
Polypropylene	3.1
SBR, SBR Latex	8.0
Acrylic Fibers	155.0
Methanol	12.9

NOTES

CHAPTER 1

1. Jacob Viner, *The Customs Union Issue* (New York: Carnegie Endowment for International Peace, 1950).

2. Tayseer A. Jaber, "The Relevance of Traditional Integration Theory to Less Developed Countries," *Journal of Common Market Studies,* IX (March, 1971): 254–67.

3. Francois Perroux, "Note sur la notion de 'pole de croissance'," as translated in *Regional Economics,* ed. David L. McKee, Robert D. Dean, and William H. Leahy (New York: Free Press, 1970): 93–103.

4. Miguel S. Wionczek, "The Rise and the Decline of Latin American Economic Integration," *Journal of Common Market Studies,* IX (September, 1970): 60.

5. These data were derived from: International Monetary Fund, *International Financial Statistics,* XXX (January 1977).

6. These data were derived from: International Monetary Fund, *International Financial Statistics,* XXX (January 1977).

7. David Morawetz, *The Andean Group: A Case Study in Economic Integration among Developing Countries.* (Cambridge: The MIT Press, 1974), p. 120.

8. This tendency of industry to concentrate in the more developed centers has been extensively analyzed in the literature. See Christopher Garbacz, *Industrial Polarization under Economic Integration in Latin America* (Austin, Texas: The University of Texas at Austin, 1971).

9. Junta del Acuerdo de Cartagena, *Grupo Andino: Primer Programa Sectorial de Desar-*

162

rollo Industrial del Sector Metalmecanico (Lima: Junta del Acuerdo de Cartagena, 1973), p. 13.

10. Alvaro Romero Galindo, *Guia de Integracion: Pacto Andino* (Bogota: Ediciones Culturales, 1974), p. 8.

11. Although the automotive program was ratified by the member countries in September 1977 by means of *Decision 120* of the Comite del Acuerdo de Cartagena, at the time of this writing it has not yet been confirmed by any of the participating countries. Furthermore, the Decision 120 does not specify a dateline for the implementation of the program and therefore it appears possible that the program will not be put into practice in the near future.

CHAPTER 2

1. C.A. Cooper and B.F. Massell, "Toward a General Theory of Customs Unions for Developing Countries," *Journal of Political Economy* 73 (October 1965): 461.

2. Ibid., p. 462.

3. See Melvyn B. Krauss, "Recent Developments in Customs Union Theory: An Interpretive Survey," *Journal of Economic Literature* X (June 1972): 413-436, for a critique of the rationale for economic integration proposed by Cooper and Massell.

4. Peter Robson, *Economic Integration in Africa* (Evanston: Northwestern University Press, 1968), p. 31.

5. Robson, *Economic Integration in Africa*, p. 33.

6. Ibid.

7. Refer to Tayseer A. Jaber, "The Relevance of Traditional Integration Theory to Less Developed Countries," *Journal of Common Market Studies* IX (March 1971): 254-267.

8. Ibid., p. 254.

9. Ibid., p. 256.

10. Ibid.

11. Jaber, "The Relevance of Traditional Integration Theory to Less Developed Countries," p. 254.

12. Walter Isard, *Methods of Regional Analysis: An Introduction to Regional Science* (Cambridge, Mass.: The M.I.T. Press, 1960), p. 233.

13. Refer to F.I. Nixson, *Economic Integration and Industrial Location: An East African Case Study* (London: Longman Group Limited, 1973), pp. 5-19.

14. Ibid., p. vii.

15. Ibid.

16. Isard, *Methods of Regional Analysis: An Introduction to Regional Science,* p. 233.

17. Refer to C.M. Heal, *The Theory of Economic Planning* (Amsterdam: North Holland Publishing Co., 1973).

18. Charles R. Blitzer, Peter B. Clark, and Lance Taylor, eds., *Economy-Wide Models and Development Planning* (London: Oxford University Press for the World Bank, 1975), pp. 33-109.

19. Refer to L.B.M. Mennes, *Planning Economic Integration Among Developing Countries* (Rotterdam: Rotterdam University Press, 1973).

20. Ibid., p. 96.

21. The discussion of these integration schemes is based on the following: David Morawetz, *The Andean Group: A Case Study in Economic Integration among Developing Countries* (Cambridge, Mass.: The M.I.T. Press, 1974), pp. 111-119; Peter Robson, *Economic*

Integration in Africa (Evanston: Northwestern University Press, 1968); Walter Krause and F. John Mathis, *Latin America and Economic Integration* (Iowa City: University of Iowa Press, 1970; F. John Mathis, *Economic Integration in Latin America: The Progress and Problems of LAFTA* (Austin, Texas: Bureau of Business Research, The University of Texas at Austin, 1969); Karel Holbik and Philip L. Swan, *Trade and Industrialization in the Central American Common Market: The First Decade,* (Austin, Texas: Bureau of Business Research, The University of Texas at Austin, 1972); and Arthur Hazelwood, *Economic Integration: The East African Experience* (New York: St. Martin's Press, 1975).

22. Robson, *Economic Integration in Africa,* p. 40.

23. Here the European Economic Community set up by the Treaty of Rome and the European Coal and Steel Community set up by the Paris Treaty are treated together as the European Common Market.

24. D.L. McLachlan and D. Swann, *Competition Policy in the European Community* (London: Oxford University Press, 1967), p. 71.

25. Ibid.

26. Ibid.

27. Ibid., p. 74.

28. Ibid., p. 77.

29. Ibid.

30. Ibid., pp. 301–326.

31. Ibid., pp. 326–359.

32. Ibid., pp. 359–380.

33. Ibid., p. 327.

34. Ibid., p. 370.

35. Holbik and Swan, *Trade and Industrialization in the Central American Common Market: The First Decade,* p. 17.

36. Wionczek, "The Rise and Decline of Latin American Economic Integration," p. 56.

37. Morawetz, *The Andean Group: A Case Study in Economic Integration Among Developing Countries,* p. 116.

38. Holbik and Swan, *Trade and Industrialization in the Central American Common Market: The First Decade,* p. 19.

39. Krause and Mathis, *Latin America and Economic Integration,* pp. 12–13.

40. Ibid., p. 13.

41. See Miguel S. Wionczek "The Rise and Decline of Latin American Economic Integration," *Journal of Common Market Studies,* IX (September 1970): 53.

42. In 1971 UDEAC was converted to Communaute Economique de l'Afrique de l'Quest (CEAO) or West African Economic Community.

43. Robson, *Economic Integration in Africa,* p. 186.

44. Ibid., p. 220.

45. Morawetz, *The Andean Group: A Case in Economic Integration among Developing Countries,* p. 112.

46. Arthur Hazlewood, *Economic Integration: The East African Experience,* p. 40.

47. Ibid., p. 72.

48. Morawetz, *The Andean Group: A Case Study in Economic Integration among Developing Countries,* p. 77.

49. Ibid.

50. Hazlewood, *Economic Integration: The East African Experience,* p. 16.

51. Refer to D.C.Mead, "The Distribution of Gains in Customs Unions between Devel-

oping Countries," in *International Economic Integration,* ed. P. Robson (Bungay, Suffolk, Great Britain: The Chaucer Press, Penguin Books, 1972), pp. 278–303.

52. Ibid., p. 291.

53. The East African Development Bank was endowed with an initial sum of capital of £ 6 million by 1969 and the total GNP of the area was about 4 billion in 1969. The source of these figures is Morawetz, *The Andean Group: A Case Study in Economic Integration Among Less Developed Countries,* pp. 111 and 113, respectively.

The Central American Common Market's initial capital was $6 million and by 1969 $69 million. The GNP of the area in 1969 was about 5 billion dollars. These figures were derived from: Holbik and Swan. *Trade and Industrialization in the Central American Common Market: The First Decade,* p. 16; and Morawetz, *The Andean Group: A Case Study in Economic Integration among Developing Countries,* p. 115.

54. Refer to I.M.D. Little, "Regional International Companies As an Approach to Economic Integration," in *International Economic Integration,* ed. P. Robson (Bungay, Suffolk, Great Britain: The Chaucer Press, Penguin Books, 1972), pp. 304–310.

55. Bela Balassa and Ardy Stoutjesdijk, "Integracion Economica de Paises en Desarrollo," *El Trimestre Economico* XLII (July–September 1975): 565–587.

56. Morawetz, *The Andean Group: A Case Study in Economic Integration among Developing Countries,* p. 83.

57. See Daniel M. Schydlowsky, "Allocating Integration Industries in the Andean Group," *Journal of Common Market Studies* IX (June 1971): 299–307.

58. Morawetz, *The Andean Group: A Case Study in Economic Integration among Developing Countries,* p. 84.

59. Ibid.

60. Schydlowsky, "Allocating Integration Industries in the Andean Group," p. 305.

61. Refer to Martin Carnoy, "A Welfare Analysis of Latin American Economic Union: Six Industry Studies," *Journal of Political Economy* 78 (July/August 1970): 626–654, and Martin Carnoy, *Industrialization in a Latin American Common Market* (Washington, D.C.: The Brookings Institution, 1972).

62. Carlos Baanante and Richard Simmons, "Effects of Customs Union on the Nitrogenous Fertilizer Industry in the Andean Zone," *Journal of Common Market Studies* XIV (March 1976): 255–275.

63. David Kendrick, "Investment Planning and Economic Integration," *Economics of Planning* VII (No. 1, 1967): 48–72.

64. Please see: Dermont Gately, "Sharing the Gains from Customs Unions among Less Developed Countries: A Game Theoretic Approach," *Journal of Development Economics* I (December 1974): 213–233.

CHAPTER 3

1. Domestic value added and international value added refer to total per unit measures of value added as will be clarified in Section IV.

2. Anne O. Krueger, "Evaluating Restrictionist Trade Regimes: Theory and Measurement," *Journal of Political Economy* 80 (January/February 1972): 54.

3. Bela Balassa and Daniel M. Schydlowsky, "Domestic Resource Costs and Effective Protection Once Again," *Journal of Political Economy* 80 (January/February 1972): 67.

4. The Balassa measure of ERP would be given as:

$$x_i^k = \frac{P_i(1 + t_i^k) - \sum_{g=1}^{H_i} a_{gi} P_g (1 + t_g^k)}{P_i - \sum_{g=1}^{H_i} a_{gi} P_g}$$

5. Balassa and Schydlowsky, "Domestic Resource Costs and Effective Protection Once Again," p. 64.

6. Bela Balassa, "Project Appraisal in Developing Countries," in *Economic Development and Planning: Essays in Honour of Jan Timbergen*, ed. by Willy Sellekaerts (White Plains, New York: International Arts and Sciences Press, Inc., 1974), p. 46.

7. This seems reasonable in view of the fact that in general there appears to be excess capacity in the industries of the LDCs and that the countries of the Andean Common Market have retained the ability to protect local industries according to the Cartagena Agreement. With respect to excess capacity and the capacity to produce more with the given resources see: Theodore Morgan, *Economic Development: Concept and Strategy* (New York: Harper and Row, Publishers, 1975), p. 331, and Harvey Leibenstein, "Allocative Efficiency vs. 'X-Efficiency,'" *American Economic Review* 56 (June 1966): 392–415.

8. Balassa and Schydlowsky, "Domestic Resource Costs and Effective Protection Once Again," p. 65.

9. Balassa and Schydlowsky, "Domestic Resource Costs and Effective Protection Once Again," p. 66.

10. See: N. R. Norman, "On the Relationship between Home-Produced and Foreign Commodities," *Oxford Economic Papers* 27 (November 1975): 426–439.

11. The symbol x_i^k is used to represent either the shadow exchange rate or the domestic resource cost of foreign exchange in industry i in country k.

If the benefits of the equation are to be equal to zero the domestic resource cost measure determines the value of the shadow exchange rate in industry i in country k.

12. For simplicity, in the formulation of these constraints only the direct contributions of capital and foreign factors, as well as the indirect contributions of these factors through the production of home good inputs, are taken into account.

13. However, if tariffs were fixed, it would be necessary to subtract from the numerator of equation 26 the savings due to economies of scale. This is not done in the empirical part of this study because of the difficulty of obtaining estimates with respect to the savings due to economies of scale.

14. See: N. R. Norman, "On the Relationship between Home-Produced and Foreign Commodities," *Oxford Economic Papers* 27 (November 1975): 426–439.

CHAPTER 4

1. The model can be applied for the allocation of industries during the formation of a common market by using the individual country pre-common market tariffs to indicate the countries' comparative advantages. The method proposed in the last chapter would not be

useful for determining the countries' comparative advantages with respect to each other in a common market with unified external tariffs.

2. Comision del Acuerdo de Cartagena, *Decision 100*, XVI Periodo de Sesiones Extraordinarias, 1976.

3. Comision del Acuerdo de Cartagena, *Decision 91*, XVII Periodo de Sesiones Ordinarias, 1975.

4. Ibid.

5. Jose Llado, *Aspectos de la Industria Petroquimica* (Madrid: Sociedad de Estudios y Publicaciones, 1962), p. 7.

6. The general characteristics of the petrochemical industry are presented in many publications. See for example: A. Lawrence Woddams, *Chemicals from Petroleum* (Pearl River, New York: The Noyes Press Inc., 1962), pp. 3–14. Asociacion Latinoamericana de Libre Comercio, *La Industria Petroquimica en la ALALC*. (ALALC/GG.PQ/I/dt 1) (1969), pp. 5–9.

7. Although the automotive program was agreed upon by the member countries in *Decision 120* of September 1977 of the Comite del Acuerdo de Cartagena, it has not yet been implemented by any of the member countries. Furthermore, the implementation of this program appears to be relegated to the distant future.

8. See A. Kuyvenhoven and L.B.M. Mennes, "Projects for Regional Co-operation," Discussion Paper No. 31, Centre for Development Planning, Erasmus University Rotterdam, March 1976.

9. Although economies of scale are considered as an important reason for selecting the petrochemical program for analysis, they are not explicitly dealt with in this study for mathematical reasons. Thus, it is implicitly assumed that economies of scale more than offset the transport costs between producing and consuming countries in order to be able to assign whole industries to the various member countries.

The above-mentioned assumption is necessary for two reasons. First, if various countries were allowed to produce the same product it would be impossible to formulate nonexclusive constraints in order to satisfy the condition that only one market be satisfied by one source. That is, it would be impossible to eliminate the possibility that one country would produce for itself and at the same time import the same product. Second, even if the problem of mutually exclusive constraints could be solved by the judicious selection of constraints, the size of the integer program to be resolved would become unmanageable given the existing solution methods for integer programming problems.

10. Junta del Acuerdo de Cartagena, *Grupo Andino: Carta Informativa Oficial* 48 (August 1975):8.

11. Junta del Acuerdo de Cartagena, *Grupo Andino: Carta Informativa Oficial* 48 (August 1975):3.

12. Junta del Acuerdo de Cartagena, *Grupo Andino: Carta Informativa Oficial* 48 (August 1975):6–7.

13. Ibid., p. 4.

14. Junta del Acuerdo de Cartagena, *Grupo Andino: Carta Informativa Oficial* 49 (September 1975):5.

15. Junta del Acuerdo de Cartagena, *Grupo Andino: Carta Informativa Oficial* 49 (September 1975):5.

16. Ibid., p. 6.

17. Ibid.

18. See: Comision del Acuerdo de Cartagena, *Decision 91*, XVIII Periodo de Sesiones Ordinarias, 1975.

19. The products were valued at 1975 international prices.

20. This information was obtained from: Comision del Acuerdo de Cartagena, *Decision 91*, XVII Periodo de Sesiones Ordinarias, 1975.

21. The allocated industries eliminated because of little or no demand are those that are nonexistent in the area and whose products are not exported from the U.S. to any of the member countries. The absence of an export entry in *U.S. Exports – Schedule B Commodity by Country* for a given product to a given country signifies that the value of the purchases of that country was less than $12,000 per year. See: U.S. Department of Commerce, Bureau of the Census, *U.S. Exports – Schedule B Commodity by Country*, FT 410, December 1974, p. X.

22. These combinations follow the industrial groupings presented in the literature. See: Frederick A. Lowenheim and Marguerite K. Moran, *Faith, Keyes and Clark's Industrial Chemicals*, 4th ed., (New York: John Wiley and Sons, 1975), and Albert V. Hahn, *The Petrochemical Industry: Market and Economics*, (New York: McGraw-Hill, 1970).

23. These figures refer to U.S. usage in 1974 and exclude exports. See: Lowenheim and Moran, *Faith, Keyes and Clark's Industrial Chemicals*, p. 393.

24. Ibid., p. 870.

25. Refer to: Hahn, *The Petrochemical Industry: Market and Economics*, p. 420.

26. The integration of the industries into more meaningful entities did not affect the JUNAC allocation very much. The changes introduced are:

a. The styrene-polystyrene industry was assigned to all countries rather than styrene to Bolivia and Venezuela and polystyrene to all.

b. The acrylic fibers, polyacrylonitrile, acrylic fiber cables, and acrylonitrile industries were assigned together to Colombia and Peru rather than separately to Colombia and Peru with the exception of acrylonitrile, which was only assigned to Peru.

c. High and low density polyethylenes were assigned to all, rather than low density to all and high density to only Bolivia, Ecuador, and Venezuela.

d. Suspension and emulsion polyvinyl chlorides were assigned to all, rather than suspension to all and emulsion only to Peru and Venezuela. The ethylene dichloride and vinyl chloride industries were assigned to all in the original allocation.

CHAPTER 5

1. The tariff schedules employed were:

1. Bolivia: Cooperativa de Artes Graficas E. Burillo Ltda., *Arancel Aduanero de Importaciones* (La Paz: Cooperativa de Artes Graficas E. Burillo Ltda., 1972).

2. Ecuador: Registro Oficial del Gobierno del Ecuador, *Ley Arancelaria y Arancel de Importacion* (Quito: Registro Oficial, 1974).

3. Chile: "Arancel de Aduanas," *Diario Oficial de la Republica de Chile* (Santiago: 9 February 1976).

4. Colombia: Gustavo Ibarra M., *Nuevo Arancel de Aduanas de Colombia* (Bogota: Legislacion Economica, on-going publication).

5. Peru: Ministerio de Economia y Finanzas, Direccion General de Aduanas, *Arancel de Aduanas del Peru*, Edicion Oficial 1973.

6. Venezuela: Legislacion Economica Ltda., *Nuevo Arancel de Aduanas de Venezuela*, (Caracas: Legislacion Economica Ltda., on-going publication).

2. This exchange was set at 11.91 Bolivian pesos per dollar. In fact, the specific duties levied by Bolivia are really expressed in dollar terms since, as established by article 16 of the *Arancel Aduanero de Importaciones,* specific duties will be readjusted for any changes in the exchange rate.

3. The exchange rates used are: Peru, 38.7 soles per dollar, and Venezuela, 5.3 bolivares per dollar.

4. The sources employed were: Stanford Research Institute, *Chemical Economics Handbook* (Stanford: Stanford Research Institute, on-going publication); *Kirk-Othmer Encyclopedia of Chemical Technology,* 2nd ed.; Asociacion Latinoamericana de Libre Comercio, *La Industria Petroquimica en la ALALC* (ALALC/GG.PQ/dt 7), 1969; *European Chemical News.*

5. Refer to U.S. Bureau of the Census, *U.S. Exports-Schedule B Commodity by Country, December 1974* (Washington, D.C.: U.S. Government Printing Office, 1975).

6. This rate was computed from information provided in Junta del Acuerdo de Cartagena, *Grupo Andino: Carta Informativa Oficial,* No. 48 (August 1975): 4-5.

7. See A.B. Woodier and J.W. Woolcock, "The ABC of the 0.6 Scale-up Factor," *European Chemical News: Large Plant Supplement,* 10 September 1965, pp. 7-9.

8. Junta del Acuerdo de Cartagena, *Grupo Andino: Carta Informativa Oficial,* No. 48 (August 1975): 4.

9. In general for a 1 percent change in the rate of return to foreign investors the DRCs change between .01 and .02 percent. Furthermore, given that in general the DRCs change in the same direction for given changes in the rate of return to foreign investment, it can be ascertained that changes in the rate of return to foreign investment have a negligible effect on industry allocations.

Specific DRCs change in opposite directions for given changes in the rate of return to foreign investment if the DRCs are respectively larger and smaller than one.

10. Refer to footnote 9.

11. Bolivia, which is landlocked, uses the Chilean port of Arica for whose use it has an agreement with Chile.

12. Naciones Unidas, Comision Economica para America Latina, *Los Fletes Maritimos en el Comercio Exterior de America Latina,* (E/CN.12/812), December 1968, p. 3.

13. Refer to Naciones Unidas, Comision Economica para America Latina, *Los Fletes Maritimos en el Comercio Exterior de America Latina,* (E/CN.12/812), December 1968.

14. Ibid.

15. This cost index is assumed to reflect only the resource costs of transportation and is not taken to be affected by demand conditions.

CHAPTER 6

1. The assignment problem can obviously also be formulated as a maximization problem.

2. Frederick S. Hillier and Gerald J. Lieberman, *Operations Research,* 2nd ed., (San Francisco: Holden-Day, Inc., 1974), p. 113.

3. In this and subsequent allocations DRCs are understood to have been computed including transport costs.

4. The solution to the problem of allocating the minimum number of industries required to fulfill the countries' minimum requirements is not considered here because it is not meaningful. In such an allocation the larger industries would invariably be excluded.

5. If the weights are constant, as they are in this work, it is possible to address the question of the size of the changes in the DRCs required for allocation changes without having to refer to the weighted DRCs since the percentage changes in the DRCs are equal to the percentage changes in the weighted DRCs.

6. The figures for the total international value added per ton in the assigned industries and figures for the marginal quantities demanded are presented in Appendix D and Table 5.01 respectively.

CHAPTER 7

1. The model has to be solved as an integer programming problem because the values of the coefficients of the decision variables in the constraints will not be limited to the values of 0 and 1, i.e., they can assume any real value.

2. Frederick S. Hillier and Gerald J. Lieberman, *Operations Research,* 2nd ed., (San Francisco: Holden-Day, Inc., 1974), p. 699.

3. Ibid., p. 698.

4. See: Egon Balas, "An Additive Algorithm for Solving Linear Programs with Zero-One Variables," *Operations Research,* 13 (July/August, 1965): 517–546; Arthur M. Geoffrion, "Integer Programming by Implicit Enumeration and Balas' Method," *SIAM Review,* 9 (April, 1967): 178–190; and Arthur M. Geoffrion, "An Improved Implicit Enumeration Approach for Integer Programming," *Operations Research,* 17 (May/June, 1969): 437–454.

5. The computer code utilized to solve the allocation model was that developed by Geoffrion and Nelson. See: A.M. Geoffrion and A.B. Nelson, "User's Instructions for 0–1 Integer Linear Programming Code RIP30C," (Santa Monica, Calif.: The Rand Corporation, 1968).

This code was made available by Dr. Alan W. Neebe of the School of Business Administration of the University of North Carolina at Chapel Hill.

The code developed by Geoffrion and Nelson was modified in two ways. First, it was redimensioned so that it would accommodate problems of the size of the allocation problem. Second, a new timing routine compatible with the computer facilities available was introduced.

6. The discussion of the Balasian algorithm is based mainly on: Hillier and Lieberman, *Operations Research,* pp. 697–721, and Geoffrion, "Integer Programming by Implicit Enumeration and Balas' Method," *SIAM Review.*

7. Note that a partial solution is not necessarily fathomed if it is infeasible: it is only fathomed when it has no feasible completions.

8. Because initially the algorithm tries to find the lowest cost solution that will satisfy the constraints, the algorithm can be expected to produce near optimal solutions even if it is terminated before all computations are completed. This point is developed later on in the chapter.

9. The discussion of surrogate constraints formulated by Geoffrion is based primarily on: A.M. Geoffrion, "An Improved Implicit Enumeration Approach for Integer Programming," *Operations Research* 17 (May/June 1969): 437–454.

10. The figures reported refer to the sum of the weighted DRCs of the 22 industries allocated in the six countries.

11. Only solutions that are better than the incumbent solutions are listed. Feasible solutions with values greater than the upper bound imposed by the best solution discovered are fathomed.

12. The figures for the percentage difference were obtained by dividing the differences between the objective functions by the averages of the objective functions.

13. The total value added in each country is given by the sum of the products of the values added in the industries assigned it and the marginal quantities demanded. For any given industry in any given country the value added per ton is equal to the product of the international value added and the DRC.

14. Although the domestic value added is a function of both demand and DRC, because the DRCs do not diverge far from the value of 1 while the demands in some industries may be several times larger than in others, the principal determinant of total domestic value added is the size of the market.

15. Loosely defined, industries demonstrating less than 5 million dollars worth of total value added are considered small. Industries with total domestic values added between 5 and 50 million are considered medium sized and those with total values added greater than 50 million are considered large.

16. Refer to Chapter V for a discussion of the relationship between the investment requirements and the volume of production in an industry.

CHAPTER 8

1. As previously mentioned, although the automotive program was ratified by the member countries in September 1977, at the time of this writing it has not yet been confirmed by any of the member countries.

2. From Table 6.01 the percentage shares of population are determined as: Bolivia 7.6%; Chile 13.8%; Colombia 31.9%; Ecuador 9.1%; Peru 21.4%; and Venezuela 16.2%.

APPENDIX A

1. Refer to Frederick A. Lowenheim and Marguerite K. Moran, *Faith, Keyes, and Clark's Industrial Chemicals*, 4th ed. (New York: John Wiley and Sons, 1975).

2. Refer to Albert V. Hahn, *The Petrochemical Industry: Market and Economics* (New York: McGraw-Hill Book Company, 1970).

3. Refer to the *Kirk-Othmer Encyclopedia of Chemical Technology*, 2nd ed.

4. Lowenheim and Moran, *Faith, Keyes, and Clark's Industrial Chemicals*, p. 207.

5. Ibid., p. 213.

6. Ibid., p. 212.

7. Ibid., p. 848.

8. Ibid., p. 608.

9. Ibid., p. 608.

10. Ibid., p. 845.

11. Ibid., p. 496.

12. Hahn, *The Petrochemical Industry: Market and Economics*, p. 360.

13. Lowenheim and Moran, *Faith, Keyes, and Clark's Industrial Chemicals*, p. 498.

14. Julius Grant, *Hack's Chemical Dictionary*, 4th ed. (New York: McGraw-Hill Book Company, 1969), p. 118.

15. Lowenheim and Moran, *Faith, Keyes, and Clark's Industrial Chemicals*, p. 184.

16. These figures were estimated from the required inputs of Butyraldehydes per ton of

butyl alcohol presented in Lowenheim and Moran, *Faith, Keyes, and Clark's Industrial Chemicals*, p. 180.

17. Ibid., p. 181.

18. Ibid., p. 398.

19. Ibid., p. 400.

20. Ibid., p. 621.

21. Hahn, *The Petrochemical Industry: Market and Economics*, p. 622.

22. These figures were estimated on the basis of the required input of cumene per ton of phenol presented in Lowenheim and Moran, *Faith, Keyes, and Clark's Industrial Chemicals*, p. 612.

23. Ibid., p. 548.

24. Ibid., p. 661.

25. Ibid., p. 810.

26. These figures were estimated on the basis of the required inputs of 2,4 tolyldiamine and phosgene presented in Lowenheim and Moran, *Faith, Keyes, and Clark's Industrial Chemicals*, p. 832.

27. Ibid., p. 202.

28. Ibid., p. 780.

29. Derived from the end-use figures presented in Hahn, *The Petrochemical Industry: Market and Economics*, p. 422.

30. Lowenheim and Moran, *Faith, Keyes, and Clark's Industrial Chemicals*, p. 782.

31. Hahn, *The Petrochemical Industry: Market and Economics*, pp. 423–424.

32. This figure was estimated on the basis of U.S. export data.

33. These figures were estimated on the basis of the required input of ethylene dichloride per ton of vinyl chloride presented in Lowenheim and Moran, *Faith, Keyes, and Clark's Industrial Chemicals*, p. 868.

34. Hahn, *The Petrochemical Industry: Market and Economics*, p. 325.

35. Ibid., p. 379.

36. Lowenheim and Moran, *Faith, Keyes and Clark's Industrial Chemicals*, p. 46.

37. Ibid., p. 524.

38. Ibid., p. 526.

BIBLIOGRAPHY

Ahmad, J. "Trade Liberalization and Structural Changes in Latin America." *Journal of Common Market Studies* XI (September 1972): 1–17.

Asociacion Latinoamericana de Libre Comercio. *La Industria Petroquimica en La ALALC* (ALALC/GG.PQ/1/dt 1) (April 1969).

Baanante, Carlos, and Simmons, Richard. "Effects of a Customs Union on the Nitrogenous Fertilizer Industry in the Andean Zone." *Journal of Common Market Studies* XIV (March 1976): 255–275.

Balas, Egon. "An Additive Algorithm for Solving Linear Programs with Zero-One Variables." *Operations Research* 13 (July–August 1965): 517–549.

Balassa, Bela. "Project Appraisal in Developing Countries." In *Economic Development and Planning: Essays in Honour of Jan Tinbergen*, pp. 40–60. Edited by Willy Sellekaerts. White Plains, New York: International Arts and Sciences Press, Inc., 1974.

———. "Regional Integration and Trade Liberalization in Latin America." *Journal of Common Market Studies* X (Sept. 1971): 58–77.

———. "Tariffs and Trade Policy in the Andean Common Market." *Journal of Common Market Studies* XII (December 1973): 176–195.

———. *The Structure of Protection in Developing Countries.* Baltimore: The John Hopkins Press, 1971.

Balassa, Bela, and Schydlowsky, Daniel M. "Domestic Resource Cost and Effective Protection Once Again." *Journal of Political Economy* 80 (January–February 1972): 63–69.

Balassa, Bela, and Schydlowsky, Daniel M. "Effective Tariffs, Domestic Cost of Foreign Exchange, and the Equilibrium Exchange Rate." *Journal of Political Economy* 76 (May–June 1968): 348–360.

Balassa, Bela, and Stoutjesdijk, Ardy. "Integracion Economica de Paises en Desarrollo." *El Trimestre Economico* XLII (July–September 1975): 565–587.

Baldwin, George B. "A Layman's Guide to Little/Mirrlees." *Finance and Development* 9 (March 1972): 16–21.

Beredjick, Nicky, ed. *Problems and Prospects of the Chemical Industries in the Less Developed Countries: Case Histories.* New York: Division of Chemical Marketing and Economics, 1970.

Blitzer, Charles R.; Clark, Peter B.; and Taylor, Lance, eds. *Economy-Wide Models and Development Planning.* London: Oxford University Press for the World Bank, 1975.

Bruno, Michael. "Domestic Resource Costs and Effective Protection: Clarification and Synthesis." *Journal of Political Economy* 80 (January–February 1972): 16–33.

Campbell, John. "A Note on Growth Poles." *Growth and Change* 2 (April 1974): 43–45.

Carnoy, Martin. "A Welfare Analysis of Latin American Economic Union: Six Industry Studies." *Journal of Political Economy* 78 (July–August 1970): 626–654.

——. *Industrialization in a Latin American Common Market.* Washington, D.C.: The Brookings Institution, 1972.

Chenery, Hollis B. "Comparative Advantage and Development Policy." *American Economic Review* 51 (March 1961): 18–51.

Chile. "Arancel de Aduanas." *Diario Oficial de la Republica de Chile.* Santiago: 9 February 1976.

Comision del Acuerdo de Cartagena. *Decisiones.* Lima: Junta del Acuerdo de Cartagena.

Cooper, C.A., and Massell, B.F. "Toward a General Theory of Customs Unions for Developing Countries." *Journal of Political Economy* 73 (October 1965): 461–476.

Cooperativa de Artes Graficas E. Burillo, Ltda. *Arancel Aduanero de Importaciones (Bolivia).* La Paz: Cooperativa de Artes Graficas E. Burillo Ltda., 1972.

Corden, W.M. "The Structure of a Tariff System and the Effective Protective Rate." *Journal of Political Economy* LXXIV (June 1966): 221–237.

Ecuador, Registro Oficial del Gobierno del Ecuador. *Ley Arancelaria y Arancel de Importacion.* Quito: Registro Oficial del Gobierno del Ecuador, 1974.

European Chemical News. Nos. published between 1965 and 1976.

Fondo de Promocion de Exportaciones. *Compilacion de Documentos Relacionados con el Acuerdo de Cartagena.* Bogota: Fondo de Promocion de Exportaciones, no date.

Garbacz, Christopher. *Industrial Polarization under Economic Integration in Latin America.* Austin, Texas: The University of Texas at Austin, 1971.

Gately, Dermont. "Sharing the Gains from Customs Unions among Less Developed Countries." *Journal of Development Economics* I (1974): 213–233.

Geoffrion, Arthur M. "An Improved Implicit Enumeration Approach for Integer Programming." *Operations Research* 17 (May–June 1969): 437–454.

——. "Integer Programming by Implicit Enumeration and Balas' Method." *SIAM Review* 9 (April 1967): 178–190.

Geoffrion, A.M., and Nelson, A.B. "Users Instructions for 0–1 Integer Linear Programming Code RIP30C." Santa Monica, Calif.: The Rand Corporation, 1968.

Gilbert, Gary G. "Investment Planning for Latin American Economic Integration." *Journal of Common Market Studies* XI (June 1973): 314–325.

Gomez Vanegas, Jorge. *Regimen del Mercado Andino*. Bogota: Legislacion Economica, Ltda., periodically updated.

Grant, Julius. *Hack's Chemical Dictionary*. 4th ed. New York: McGraw-Hill Book Company, 1969.

Hahn, Albert V. *The Petrochemical Industry: Market and Economics*. New York: McGraw-Hill Book Company, 1970.

Happel, John, and Jordan, Donald G. *Chemical Process Economics,* 2nd ed. New York: Marcel Dekker, Inc., 1975.

Hazlewood, Arthur. *Economic Integration: The East African Experience*. New York: St. Martin's Press, 1975.

Heal, G.M. *The Theory of Economic Planning*. Amsterdam: North-Holland Publishing Company, 1973.

Hillier, Frederick S., and Lieberman, Gerald J. *Operations Research*. 2nd ed. San Francisco: Holden-Day, Inc., 1974.

Holbik, Karel, and Swan, Philip L. *Trade and Industrialization in the Central American Common Market: The First Decade*. Austin, Texas: Bureau of Business Research, The University of Texas at Austin, 1969.

Ibarra M., Gustavo. *Nuevo Arancel de Aduanas de Colombia*. Bogota: Legislacion Economica, periodically updated.

International Monetary Fund. *International Financial Statistics* XXX (January 1977).

Isard, Walter. *Methods of Regional Analysis: An Introduction to Regional Science*. Cambridge, Mass.: The M.I.T. Press, 1960.

Jaber, Tayseer A. "The Relevance of Traditional Integration Theory to Less Developed Countries." *Journal of Common Market Studies* IX (March 1971): 254–167.

Junta del Acuerdo de Cartagena. *Grupo Andino: Carta Informativa Oficial*. Lima: Junta del Acuerdo de Cartagena.

——. *Grupo Andino: Primer Programa Sectorial de Desarrollo Industrial del Sector Metalmecanico*. Lima: Junta del Acuerdo de Cartagena, 1973.

Kendrick, David. "Investment Planning and Economic Integration." *Economics of Planning* VII No. 1 (1970): 48–72.

Kirk-Othmer Encyclopedia of Chemical Technology. 2nd ed.

Krause, Walter, and Mathis, F. John. *Latin America and Economic Integration*. Iowa City: University of Iowa Press, 1970.

Krauss, Melvyn B. "Recent Developments in Customs Union Theory: An Interpretive Survey." *Journal of Economic Literature* X (June 1972): 413–436.

Krueger, Anne O. "Evaluating Restrictionist Trade Regimes: Theory and Measurement." *Journal of Political Economy* 80 (January–February 1972): 48–62.

Kuyvenhoven, A., and Mennes, L.B.M. "Projects for Regional Co-operation." Discussion Paper No. 31, Centre for Development Planning, Erasmus University Rotterdam, March 1976.

Lal, Deepak, *Methods of Project Analysis: A Review.* Washington, D.C.: International Bank for Reconstruction and Development, 1974.

Legislacion Economica, Ltda. *Nuevo Arancel de Aduanas de Venezuela.* Caracas: Legislacion Economica, periodically updated.

Little, I.M.D. "Regional International Companies as an Approach to Economic Integration." In *International Economic Integration,* pp. 304–310. Edited by P. Robson. Bungay, Suffolk, Great Britain: The Chaucer Press, Penguin Books, 1972.

Llado, Jose. *Aspectos de la Industria Petroquimica.* Madrid: Sociedad de Estudios y Publicaciones, 1962.

Lowenheim, Frederick A., and Moran, Marguerite K. *Faith, Keyes and Clark's Industrial Chemicals.* 4th ed. New York: John Wiley and Sons, 1975.

McLachlan, D.L., and Swann, D. *Competition Policy in the European Community.* London: Oxford University Press, 1967.

Manne, Alan S. "Multi-Sector Models for Development Planning: A Survey." *Journal of Development Economics* 1 (1974): 43–69.

Mathis, F. John. *Economic Integration in Latin America: The Progress and Problems of LAFTA.* Austin, Texas: Bureau of Business Research, The University of Texas at Austin, 1969.

Mead, D.C. "The Distribution of Gains in Customs Unions between Developing Countries." In *International Economic Integration,* pp. 278–303. Edited by P. Robson. Bungay, Suffolk, Great Britain: The Chaucer Press, Penguin Books, 1972.

Mennes, L.B.M. *Planning Economic Integration among Developing Countries.* Rotterdam: Rotterdam University Press, 1973.

Morawetz, David. "Harmonization of Economic Policies in Customs Unions: The Andean Group." *Journal of Common Market Studies* XI (June-1973): 294–313.

——. *The Andean Group: A Case Study in Economic Integration among Developing Countries.* Cambridge, Mass.: The M.I.T. Press, 1974.

Morgan, Theodore. *Economic Development: Concept and Strategy.* New York: Harper and Row, Publishers, 1975.

Naciones Unidas, Comision Economica para America Latina. *Los Fletes Maritimos en el Comercio Exterior de America Latina* (E/CN.12/812) (December 1968).

Nixson, F.I. *Economic Integration and Industrial Location: An East African Case Study.* London: Longman Group Limited, 1973.

Norman, N.R. "On the Relationship between Prices of Home-Produced and Foreign Commodities." *Oxford Economic Papers* 27 (November 1975): 426–439.

Noyes, Robert. *World Petrochemical Report.* Pearl River, New York: Noyes Research Company, 1964.

Perroux, Francois. "Note on the Concept of Growth Poles." Translated by Linda Gates and Anne Marie McDermott. In *Regional Economics: Theory and Practice,* pp. 93–103. Edited by David L. McKee, Robert D. Dean, and William H. Leahy. New York: The Free Press, 1970.

Peru, Ministerio de Economia y Finanzas, Direcion General de Aduanas. *Arancel de Aduanas del Peru.* Edicion Oficial, 1973.

Robson, Peter. *Economic Integration in Africa.* Evanston: The Northwestern University Press, 1968.

——. "The Distribution of Gains in Customs Unions between Developing Countries: A Note." *KYKLOS-International Review for Social Sciences* XXIII No. 1 (1970): 117–119.

Romero Galindo, Alvaro. *Guia de Integracion: Objectivos y Realizaciones del Pacto Andino.* Bogota: Ediciones Culturales, no date.

Schydlowsky, Daniel M. "Allocating Integration Industries in the Andean Group." *Journal of Common Market Studies* IX (June 1971): 299–307.

Stanford Research Institute. *Chemical Economics Handbook.* Stanford: Stanford Research Institute, periodically updated.

U.S. Bureau of the Census. *U.S. Exports-Schedule B Commodity by Country, December 1974.* Washington, D.C.: Government Printing Office, 1975.

U.S. Department of Commerce. *Survey of Current Business.*

Viner, Jacob. *The Customs Union Issue.* New York: Carnegie Endowment for International Peace, 1950.

Wagner, Harvey M. *Principles of Operations Research.* Englewood Cliffs, New Jersey: Prentice-Hall, Inc., 1969.

Wionczek, Miguel S. "The Rise and Decline of Latin American Economic Integration." *Journal of Common Market Studies* IX (September 1970): 49–66.

Woodier, A.B., and Woolcock, J.W. "The ABC of the 0.6 Scale-Up Factor," *European Chemical News: Large Plant Supplement* (10 September 1965): 7–9.